TaxiTutor™: Classroom Edition

INTERNET-CHINESE™
LANGUAGE COMPANION™

Speak Mandarin

说 京 话 ⇔ Shuo Jinghuaa

SPEAK ENGLISH

⇔ 说 英 语 ⇔

SHUO YINGYYUU

PINXXIEE PRESS USA

www.InternetChinese.com

Dr. TiEN's
Mandarin-Chinese®
LANGUAGE COMPANION™

H. C. Tien, M.D. 田三文 Tiann San Wenn

An Internet-Chinese MANDARIN Tutorial

ISBN: 0-9714824-2-X
Published in the United States of America by
PINXXIEE PRESS

PINXXIEE® Trademark Reg. U.S. Patent Office and China Patent Office

China Patent Number: 88 1 02009.5 & U.S. Patent Number: 5,257,938

CHINA Certificate of Standardization ® 1999 CSA [1990] ZBXFMZ [1990] 032

NB: The first fragment of the Pinxxiee 'Rosetta Stone' was discovered in East Lansing, Michigan, 1960. The derived Pinxxiee Language Technology papers have been published and copyrighted in WJP [World Journal of Psychosynthesis] and duly copyright © 1961-2001, periodically, under: Library of Congress Catalog Card Number 70-111300.

For more information, write to the Publisher:

PINXXIEE PRESS
All Rights Reserved
Under Bern and Pan-American Copyright Convention
All communications should be directed to:
ccc@pinxxiee.com

Printed in USA

For Audrey Roberts,
My Life-Long Traveling Companion with

Her Motto in Welsh:

MWYNHAU BYWYD^{cymraeg}

.

INTRODUCTION

The Internet-Chinese Language Companion™ is based on The Internet-Chinese TaxiTutor®, which is a lively conversational tutorial, shared between a Beijing Mandarin-speaking taxi driver and his English-speaking foreign traveler. They teach each other in a fast-moving experimental language laboratory, the TAXICAB!

The *Language Companion*™ is written in three scripts _and_ also in 3 columns, _Internet-English_ [first column], _Internet-Chinese_ [second column] and _square Chinese characters_ [third column].
By *Internet-English*, we mean English often spoken at international airports. It is a kind of Airport-English. This is to keep the sentences concise and in a natural Internet-literal order. What does this mean? That is, we typically use the basic word order of _subject - verb - object,_ e.g. *'you-speak-English.'* And ask questions in the same word order. Try the 3 contrived examples in Internet-English, Internet-Chinese and Internet-French:

'[Do] you speak English?' = 'Nniij shuo Yingyyuu?' = 'Vous parlez Anglais?'

This speaking order accelerates bilingual learning by the neuro-association of phonics with graphics, sound with writing, promoting unconscious vocabulary building, by way of natural left brain ⇔ right brain information transfer between two brain hemispheres and two languages. And between two scripts, phonic and graphic, as represented by English and Chinese, respectively.

This Chinese *Language Companion* ™ empowers you to speak Mandarin with any Mandarin-Chinese speaker, for example a Beijing taxi driver. Mastering this booklet enables you and the driver to respond in simple American-Chinese dialogue. And so, take this booklet along with you on your trip to China. You can read and enjoy it during your long *flight* over. This *Language Companion* ™ course can be recycled weekly, with a tourist guide, a company trainer or a school instructor for week-long Chinese language program. Of course, you can learn by *yourself* and start an Internet-Chinese TaxiTutor™ class with a Mandarin-speaking friend, and play act the dialogue tutorial, dramatizing the story of a Mobile Language laboratory as if in the actual Beijing streets, the People's Republic of China.

'[Do] You speak English?' = 'Nniij shuovz Yingyyuu?' = '你 说 英语？'

INTERNET-CHINESE LANGUAGE COMPANION ™ TAXITUTOR®		
Internet-English	Internet-Chinese	Chinese Characters
Author	Zuoojia	作家
Dr. Tien	Tiann San Wenn	田三文
CHINESE LANGUAGE COMPANION ™ AUDIOCASSETTE		
Interpreters	Fanyiiyuann	翻译员
Gareth Tien	Tiann Yih Zzevvt	田一泽
Jiao Jing	Jiaojl Jiinghhlh	焦 静
Project Programmer		
Michael Nation	Maikeer Naaixiing	麦克尔.耐 兴
Requested by the Michigan-Beijing Network		
Evelyn C. Spears	Yifulin C. Sipiersi	伊夫林.斯尔皮 尔斯
For Non-Governmental Organization Forum on Women Attending 1995		
United Nations 4th World Conference On Women	Liannhhegguo Diisii Jieephj Fuunneuu Daaibbiaao Daahuii	联合 国 第 四 届 妇女 代表 大会
Beijing, China	Bbeeijing, ZhongGguo	北京,中国

RECOGNITION

MANY THANKS TO CHINESE-ENGLISH TRANSLATION FRIENDS, BRIDGING EAST-WEST:
Please Share This Special Recognition for

**Gareth, Chinese-English Pinxxiee Translator
[Tiann Yih Zzes]
With His Dignified Personality and Lifelong Contributions
Developing East-West Communications and
In Promoting U.S.-China Peoples Friendship**

**Ddaxiee: Yih Zzes, Zhong-Ying Fanyii Pinxxiee Yuannd
[Gareth Roberts Tien]
Genjuu Tay Gaoshaangde Renngge jji Yishengde Goongxiaan
Fazhaannzhe Dong-Xih Xiinxi Jiaolliu hhe
Cuujiin Zhong-Mmeei Rennminn Yyoouyii**

答谢:一泽,中英拼写翻译员
[Gareth]
根据 他 高尚的 人 格及一生的 贡献
发展着 东-西 信息交流 和
促进中-美 人民 友谊

ACKNOWLEDGMENT

I would like to express my sincere appreciation to:

Madame Chai 柴夫人 and **Ambassador Chai Zemin 柴泽民 大使,
First Chinese Ambassador to the United States of America;

And

Mrs. Sharon Woodcock and **Ambassador Leonard Woodcock伍德科克大使,
First American Ambassador to the People's Republic of China,

Good wishes to the new 'people's ambassadors' going to the East.

With goodwill and knowledge, in a way, every traveler to another nation,
Serves as a cultural ambassador from one's homeland. This Booklet,
Your *Mandarin-Chinese Language Companion,* having served Michigan Women
attending 1995 United Nations 4th World Conference on Women in Beijing,
will now serve as your Interpreter and translator,
on your journey to my hometown.

**For their encouragement in 1970's for my early Computer-Chinese R&D on
Tenstrokes Pinxxiee (Pinyin+Pindiaao+Pinxinng) and their continuing support ever
since for the resultant Internet-Chinese language projects, that produced this booklet,
Mandarin-Chinese Language Companion for current and future tourists and
businesspeople, traveling East and West.

Wishing you in three scripts:

A Journey of Safety! Yih Luu Pinng An! 一路平安！

Dr. Tien/Tiann San Wenn/田三文
East Lansing, Michigan, USA 2001

TRILINGUAL RENDITION OF ACKNOWLEDGEMENT		
INTERNET-ENGLISH	INTERNET-CHINESE	CHINESE CHARACTERS
I would like to express my sincere appreciation to :	Wwooj gaoxiingdi bbiaaodda wwoode chenngzhii gaannxiee zhiiyx:	我高兴地表达我的诚挚感谢 致:
Mrs. Sharon Woodcock and Ambassador Leonard Woodcock,	Sharon Woodcock furenn hhe Leonard Woodcock Daashhii,	沙伦伍德科克夫人和伦纳德,伍德科克大使,
First American Ambassador to	Diiyireen Mmeeigguo zhuupzt	第一任美国驻
the People's Republic of China	Zhonghhua Rennminn Goonghhegguo	中华人民共和国
and	hhe	和
Madame Chai and Ambassador Chai Zemin,	Chhaitv Furenn hhe Chhaitv Zzes Min Daashhii,	柴夫人和柴泽民大使,
First Chinese Ambassador to	Diiyih reen ZhongGguo Daashhii	第一任中国大使
the United States of America	zhuupzt Mmeeiliijian Goonghhegguo	驻美利坚共和国
and	hhe	和
good wishes to the new travelers	hhaaode zhuuyuaan zhiiyx xinde lleuukee	好的祝愿致心的旅客
to the Land of Cathay, visited by	qiannwaanng Shennzhou,	前往神州,
Marco Polo centuries ago.	Marco Polo cenngjing yyoulaann guoode jjii bbaai niann qiann.	马尔科波洛 Marco Polo 曾经游览过的几百年前.
In a way, every traveler to another nation, like Marco Polo	Rruccii, mmeeiy yih gee lleuuyouzhhee canguan, bbiirru	如此,每一个旅游者参观, 比如马尔科波洛 [Marco Polo]
Serves as a cultural ambassador	zuoowwei yigee wennhuaa Ambassador	做为一个文化大使
from one's homeland.	conng ziijjiie jiaxiang.	从自己的家乡.
As author of the Language Companion,	Chenngwwei Mmeei-Hhua Yyuuyann Baanlleuu de zuoojia,	成为美-华语言伴侣的作家,
I am delighted to serve as your	Wwooj feichanng gaoxiingdi	我非常高兴地
interpreter and translator via	ffuwuu, wwei nniimende jjieeshuo yuannd yoong	服务,为你们的翻译员用
booklet and the audiocassette,	zhee xxiaao ceezi hhe luuyindaai.	这小册子和录音带.
on your journey to Beijing,	dang nnii lleuuyyou quu Bbeeijing,	当你旅游去北京,
my home town.	wwoode llaao jiaxiang.	我的老家乡.
Wishing you	Zhuuvplv ninn	祝您
A Safe Trip All the Way!	Yih Luu Pinng An!	一路平安!
Dr. Tien, Michigan 1995	Tiann San Wenn, Michigan 1995	田三文,密西根 1995

PRONUNCIATION GUIDE
Mandarin Chinese = PpuuTongHuaa

The *Language Companion* ™ has three (3) basic Rules:
<u>Rule 1.</u> Speak Mandarin-Chinese;
<u>Rule 2.</u> Spell Mandarin-Chinese; and
<u>Rule 3.</u> Write Mandarin-Chinese.

What's Mandarin-Chinese? It is not Cantonese, not Shanghainese, nor any other of the 50 or so dialects of China. Practically speaking, Mandarin-Chinese is Beijing Dialect, and its Internet-Chinese™ spelling is now standardized and known to Chinese-speaking people all over the world, on or off the Net, as <u>General Speech</u> [*P ŭ- t ōng- hu à* , 普-通-话], using the Pinyin Alphabet, as approved by the Chinese People's government in 1958 and accepted by the United Nations as China's phonic standard in 1979.

<u>Rule1.</u> Speak Mandarin. <u>Action:</u> *Pronounce every Pinyin syllable, as spelled out with toneletters* (not with silent tonemarks like - / V \ over the vowels u, o, a, as used in 'P ŭ - t ōng- hu à '; or with numbers 1 2 3 or 4, as in 'Pu-3 tong-1 hua4'. Toneletters *form a natural sound stream* (using letters) Ppuu-Tong-Huaa → Ppuutonghuaa': This is the modernized Internet-Chinese spelling, which is based firmly on standard Chinese Phonetic Scheme [Haanyyuu Pinyin FangAan, 汉语拼音方案] for current direct e-mail applications like Internet-English script. There are tones in Mandarin, as there are accents in English. There are 4 basic tones to each Mandarin syllable; for example, the Pinyin syllable <u>ma</u> has 4 tones, ma-1, ma-2, ma-3 and ma-4. Try to learn from your taxi driver or from a Mandarin-speaking friend: Do practice the 4 tones! You need to master the 4 tones. Why? Here is a funny example:
"Ma-1 ma-4 ma-3!" meaning "Mom curses horse!", but
"Ma-3 ma-4 ma-1!", meaning "Horse curses Mom!"
And you will have a hilarious time, talking with your taxi driver. Have confidence, and help is coming! It is the *Language Companion* ™.

Language Companion ™ offers service with the Internet-Chinese alphabetic script (for details, refer to Appendix: Internet-Chinese Pinxxiee Orthography) . With an alphabetic type of writing and spelling, you will have a much better chance of remembering 'Haanzii=Ideograph' rather than the traditional Chinese *square* ideographs of '汉字'='Sinograph'. Yet reading the same Internet-Chinese word 'Haanzii' is equivalent in writing the inscrutable Chinese characters like 汉字. 'Haanzii' reads like an English word or a linearized 'Chinese ideograph' or 'Sinograph'. Your taxi driver likewise can start learn English with an alphabetic script. An Internet-Chinese script will help everybody, native and foreigners alike. Everybody can learn speak Mandarin more correctly; and as a bonus, gaining an ability to write Chinese e-mail with more accuracy and efficiency with an Internet-alphabetized Chinese *linear* script. This program will make up lost time and earn more money, for both the rider-customer and the cab driver in the long run. An enlightening *Journey to the East* awaits you with this NEW INTERNET-CHINESE

SCRIPT: Astonishingly, learning Internet-Chinese means mastering the beautiful Chinese ideographs (square sinography) as well! That is, with the touch of a keystroke and using TaxiTutor conversion software, can you change and transform the following sample phrase: 'Internet-Chinese Writes Ideographs!' from a modernized readable Chinese script to the inscrutable classical characters on request:

Internet-Zhongwenn xxiee Haanzii! ⇔ 因特网 -中 文 写 汉 字！

Rule 2. Spell Mandarin: <u>Action:</u> *Use Pinyin+toneletters+stroke-letters formula*: **Pinyin is the modern Chinese phonetic alphabet, mandated by China in 1958 and accepted by the United Nations in 1979. Both Pinyin and English alphabet use the same 26 Latin letters. Almost all Mandarin vowels and consonants are pronounced *similarly* to English. <u>All consonants except these 4 letters, C R Q X</u> <u>[mnemonic: crux]</u>:**

<u>*C R Q X are pronounced differently from English:*</u>
<u>*Note c = ts, r = zsur, q = chee, x = shee. c r q x,*</u>

Internet-Chinese uses Pinyin+Toneletters to spell Mandarin as the standard dialect. The toneletters separate Chinese homophones for uniqueness, efficiency and meaning. [It's not unlike spelling English homophones with extra letters to separate *to, too,* and *two* from each other.] Let's take three syllables, *ma, man* and *wo* as examples. The 4 tones for <u>*ma*</u> or <u>*man*</u> or <u>*wo*</u> in Mandarin must be similarly spelled out in 4 different ways, in order to be written obviously and therefore easily sounded out clearly, as in the three examples, like so:
ma (mom), mma (hemp), mmaa (horse), and maa (curse); or
man (savage), mann (dupe), maann (filled), and maan (slow) or
wo (nest), wwo (no meaning), wwoo (I-or-me), and woo (fertile).
Now, you can see Mandarin <u>toned</u> syllables spelled precisely and read distinctly in its Internet-Chinese script.

Rule 3. Write Mandarin Chinese: <u>Action:</u> *E-mail in Internet-Chinese Script:* **That is, write Internet-Chinese words, like some English words, e.g. 'hi <u>gh</u>', 'throu<u>gh</u>', 'wei<u>gh</u>', as if it were linearized "square" Chinese characters with silent consonants. The silent consonant letters usually occur at the end of a word. For example, an Internet-Chinese word model: The pronoun "I-or-me" = " 我 " is <u>*simplified & linearized*</u> into an Internet-Chinese word:**
"wo + toneletters + j-stroke" = " *wo+ wo + j* " = wwooj.
Quietly observe *the End-consonants rule*[1]. Don't pronounce the consonant letter, -*j* being the silent first stroke of this Chinese character, which you can now decode into TiENSTROKES letters. But do remember only in 5% of Internet-Chinese

---

[1]The End-consonants Rule: The end-consonants actually represent the initial silent *graphic* (not phonic) stroke-letters of the original Chinese ideograms, especially in people's names or in poetry or monosyllabic words. If puzzled as to why these silent stroke-letters must persist in the modern Internet-Chinese words, then you may wish to read and enjoy the ancient **Chinese Homophone Enigma** and its modern **Sinographic TiENSTROKES Solution.**
[For details, see Appendices, INTERNET-CHINESE PINXXIEE SCRIPT: Theory & Practice]

⊞™ TiENSTROKES ® USA
www. internetchinese.com * China Certificate of Standardization®1999 * www.tienstrokes.com

words, like "*wwooj*" the silent stroke letters are added. Why add silent letters? ANSWER: Because "*wwooj*" IS the modern linearized form of the ideograph " 我 "! "*Wwooj*" has therefore both the phonic 'wwoo-' *and* the graphic letter '-j', the first stroke of the ideograph. By physical analogy, the ideograph " 我 " is an ice-cube; decoded to "j-hjtgjv" ,the string of strokeletters *as the melting water, and "wwooj" is the energized steam. All 3 are basically made of H2O, the same water molecules in 3 physical states. Continuing this analogy, "我" or "j-hjtgjv" or "wwooj" are all of the same basic Chinese graphiphonic elements for the English idea-words of "I-or-me".* Think through the unifying idea of the 3 scripts. You will master the know-how in speaking, spelling and writing e-mails in the modernized Internet-Chinese script, as easily as in the Internet-English script on the WWW:

WorldWideWeb = WaanWweiWaanng = 万维网.

Knowing the three basic Internet-Chinese Rules, you are ready to sound out correctly any Mandarin-Chinese word. And again, let's emphasize this modernized language technology, as you are actually speaking Mandarin accurately with any Mandarin-Chinese speaker, again for example, a Beijing taxi driver and acquiring an extra ability to e-mail directly in modern Internet-Chinese script, like the Internet-English script on the Net: like so:

[do] You speak English? = Nniij shuo Yingyyuu? = <u>Nniij shuo Yingyyuu?</u>
I speak Mandarin-Chinese. = Wwooj shuo Bbeeijinghuaa. = 我 说 北 京 话.
Ahoy, Good! = Aiya, Hhaao! = 哎呀, 好!

Why write the Internet-Chinese phrase <u>Nniij shuo Yingyyuu?</u> twice on the above paragraph? *For dramatic demo*: By pressing a computer button with an Internet-Chinese conversion software, the second linearized Internet-Chinese words will automatically become the corresponding unique square Chinese characters. Why convert them? Answer: For people who don't know Internet-Chinese script and/or cannot read Internet-English script, either. (Now, pretend pushing a button on an e-mail line below:

[Do] You speak English? = Nniij shuo Yingyyuu? = <u>Nniij shuo Yingyyuu?</u>
You speak English? = Nniij shuo Yingyyuu? ⇔ 你 说 英 语?
Similarly,
I speak Mandarin-Chinese. = Wwooj shuo Bbeeijinghuaa. = 我 说 北 京 话.

Ahoy, Good! = Aiya, Hhaao! = 哎呀, 好!

Therefore, the main text of this *Language Companion* is written in this trilingual format. The exciting discovery is the 'linearization of square Chinese script' into an Internet-Chinese script. It is very similar to English script. It is equivalent to the traditional 'square sinography'. If you master the modernized linear Internet-Chinese writing for writing e-mail, you have also learned how to e-mail in the traditional Chinese characters!

A Beijing Taxi Driver may simply ask you A KEY QUESTION:
"Which script you can read right away?"

Aiya, Hhaao! or 哎呀, 好! [Ahoy, Good!]

Translation Guide

[1] **The purpose of** Internet-Chinese *Language Companion* ™ is to serve travelers and students as *an accelerated learning system*. Its trilingual format as shown in the basic 10 lessons has 3 scripts in 3 columns: *Internet-English, Internet-Chinese and Chinese characters* (Square Sinography).

INTERNET-ENGLISH	INTERNET-CHINESE	SQUARE SINOGRAPHY
[Do] You speak English?	Nnii shuo Yingyyuu?	你 说 英语?
[Do] You speak Mandarin?	Nnii shuo Jinghuaa?	你 说 京 话?
Yes, I can.	Shiide, wwoo huii.	是的, 我 会.

[2] **The standard sentence structure of** *Language Companion* uses a simple order, namely *subject-verb-object: You-speak-English = Nnii-shuo-Yingyyuu*

In Internet-Chinese Language Companion, most of its translation text attempts to match up pronouns, verbs, nouns, etc., as in the above example, so that word-for-word translation, *you-speak-English?* matches word-for-word Internet-Chinese sentence, *Nnii-shuo-Yingwenn?* Hence the name: Internet-English. The English idiomatic [Do] is bracketed off, so the beginner can quickly learn by association, you=nnii, speak=shuo, English=Yingyyuu, as spelled in Internet-Chinese. But what is Internet-Chinese?

[3] The Internet-Chinese script is the one-to-one, graphic-to-phonic, character-for-word transformation of the traditional *square* Chinese Characters. This transformation is the *linearized* equivalent in a modernized Internet-Chinese script. That is, translate another English sentence, *for example,* "You speak Mandarin? " not directly into Chinese Characters " 你 说 京 话?" Since you may not able to read these ideographs (unless you spend many years of learning them). The GOOD NEWS is that Internet-Chinese is plainly readable as you speak in Mandarin, and moreover automatically convertible into Chinese characters:

Nnii shuo Jinghuaa=你 说 京 话?

ORIGIN OF THE INTERNET-CHINESE SCRIPT: This script is based on Chinese Government 's 1958 Mandarin Phonetic System[2], Dr. Tien further developed it and tested in six Beijing Elementary and Middle Schools, from 1995-2001, using Internet-Chinese = Pinyin + 4-Tones + 10-Strokes = Pinxxiee = Linearized Chinese Characters or Pinxxiee Script [Beijing Pinxxiee Report][3]. In 1999, CAS (China Standardization Association) certified Internet-Chinese as an alternate e-script to the Chinese Characters. CAS promoted it as an efficient tool for Mandarin speakers to write e-mail like in English. Internet-Chinese is a *fast* learning tool.

---

[2] Refer to Mandarin Phonetic System = Haanyyuu Pinyin FangAan: Xinhua Dictionary with English Translation, The Commercial Press International Co., LTD. 2000]

[3] Refer to Beijing Pinxxiee Report, translated by Gareth R. Tien, 1996, pp 81-83,

AN INTRODUCTORY STORY
Dialogue Between A Chinese Taxi Driver
And An American Jet Traveler

Special Note: Column 1 *tells the complete story. One or two English words in each phrase are introduced and underlined (like* Hello!*). Column 2* shows the modernized Internet-Chinese translation of the selected word (Halluo!)*. For those interested in the traditional Chinese characters,* Column 3 *shows the equivalent (*哈罗!*)*
This "tri-lingual" approach is used throughout the book.

	Column 1	Column 2	Column 3
	INTERNET-ENGLISH	INTERNET-CHINESE	汉字
TT:	**Taxi Tutor =TT:** Waiting in front of Beijing Airport.	**Chuzuche Zhuujiaao = CZ**	出租车 助教
JT	**Jet Traveler =JT:** Coming out of Beijing Airport.	**Pensheeji Lleuukee = PL**	喷射机旅客
TT:	**Hello!**	**Halluo!**	哈罗!
JT	You speak **English!**	**Yingyyuu!**	英语!
TT	**Yes**, I'm a Mandarin TaxiTutor.	**Shiide**	是的
JT	What do **you** do?	**Nnii** gan shennme?	你干甚么?
TT	**I am** a Taxi Driver, able to speak a little English. This is my Taxi Company's policy.	**Wwoo(j) shii** Takeesi Siji,	我是他客司驾驶员,
JT	You are **for hire?**	Nnii kkeeyyii **chuzu?**	你可以出租?
TT	Yes, of course (opening car door), **please** get in.	Shiide, dangrann (ddaakaizhe chemenn), **qiinng** shaang.	是的,当然(打开 — — 车门),请上.
JT	(sitting in the cab) **How are you?**	(Zuozaai che shaang) **Nnii hhaao ma?**	(坐在车上)你 — — 吗?
TT	**Good, thanks.** To where?	**Hhaao, xieexiee.** Quu nnaar?	好,谢谢. 去哪儿?
JT:	**Beijing Hotel.**	**Bbeeijing Faandiaan.**	北京饭店.
TT	**Mandarin** is 'Bbeeijing Faandiaan'.	**Jinghuaa** shii 'Bbeeijing Faandiaan'.	京话是 '北京— —店'.
JT:	Oh, *'faandiaan'* **means** *'hotel'?* And how do you spell it?	Ah, *'Faandiaan'* **yiisi** shii *'Hotel'?*	啊,'饭店' **意思** 是 '旅馆'?
TT:	**Correct.** And, we are spelling out *the tones in 'f*à n di à n*'*: like so: *'f a a n d i a a n'*. Now clearly, we can spell out tones with letters of the alphabet.	**Duii.**	对.
JT:	**Very good!** When did you learn the English alphabet?	**Heenn hhaao!**	很好!
TT:	**First grade.**	**Yih niannjji.**	一年级.

www. internetchinese.com * China Certificate of Standardization®1999 * www.tienstrokes.com

JT:	So early!?	Zheeme zzaao!?	这么早!?
TT:	Yes, **my teacher** called it the Chinese Pinyin Alphabet.	Shiide, **wwoode llaaoshi**	是的,我的 老师
JT:	**Pinyin Alphabet** is like the English Alphabet?	**Pinyin Ziimmuu**	拼音字母
TT:	Yes, Pinyin has the **same** 26 Latin letters. All sound like English letters, except for four.	Shiide, Pinyin yyoou **yiyaangde** 26 gee Lading ziimmuu.	是的,拼音 有 一样的 26 个拉丁 字母.
JT:	**Which four** Mandarin letters sound different from English?	**Nnaa sii gee**	哪四个
TT:	'C', 'R', 'Q' & ' X'.	'C', 'R', 'Q' & ' X'.	'C', 'R', 'Q' & ' X'.
JT:	How do 'C R Q X' **letters** sound in Mandarin?	'C R Q X' **ziimmuu**	'C R Q X' 字母
TT:	'C' & 'R' are **similar** to English.	'C' &'R' shii **leeisi**	'C' &'R' 是类似
JT:	**Then** 'Q' & 'X' ?	**Naame** 'Q' & 'X' ?	那么 'Q' & 'X'?
TT:	'Q' **sounds** like 'chee' as in 'cheese'.	'Q' **fayin** 'chee'	'Q'发音 像 'chee'
JT:	The **letter** 'X'?	**Ziimmuu** 'X' ne?	字母 'X' 呢?
TT:	'X' **sounds** like 'she' as in 'Sheila'.	'X' **fayin** 'she'	'X' 发音 'she'
JT	**Where** do I get a reference **book**?	**Nnaar** qquu yih beenn cankkaao **shu**?	哪儿取 一本 参考 书?
TT:	**Here is** my book on TaxiTutor.	**Zheer shii**	这儿是
JT:	**Very interesting**. Where did you get it? (Noticing TaxiTutor's 3 scripts: English, Internet-Chinese and Square Characters.)	**Heenn yyoouyiisi**. Nnii nnaar qquu daao de?	很有意思.你 一 亩一取到的?
TT:	My cab **company's** English training department.	Wwoode Chuzuche **Gongsi**	我的 出租车 公司
JT	**Where** can I get a copy?	**Nnaar**	哪儿?
TT:	You can have my **copy**.	Nnii kkeeyyii ddedaao wwoode **kkaaobeei**.	你可以 得到我的 拷 贝.
JT:	Oh, **many thanks**.	Ah, **duo xiee**.	啊,多谢.
TT:	**Arrived:** Bbeeijing Faandiaan. (Arrived at Peking Hotel)	**Daaole:** Bbeeijing Faandiaan. (Daaole Peking Hotel)	到了:北京饭店.(到了北京饭店)
JT:	**How much money?**	**Duoshhaao qiannj?**	多少钱?
TT:	Pay according to **taximeter**.	Aanzhaao **Takeesi Jiijiaaqii**.	按照他客司 记价器.
JT:	**Please** keep the change.	**Qiinng** lliuxiaa linngqiann.	请 留下 零钱.
TT:	**Thank you.**	**Xieexiee nnii.**	谢谢 你.

JT:	**Tomorrow** can you take me sightseeing, around Beijing, starting at 8 am, from here?	**Minngtian** nnii nennggoou …	明天你能够…
TT:	**I can.** A whole day?	**Wwooj nenng.** Yih zheenng tian?	我能.一 整 天？
JT:	Yes. And **teach me** Mandarin-Chinese Lesson 2?	Shiide. Biing **jiaoh wwooj**	是的.并教我
TT:	I will be **very happy** to teach you Mandarin. Please bring the book, TaxiTutor along. And you can tutor me English, too! **See** [you] tomorrow.	Wwooj **feichanng gaoxiing** Minngtian **jiaan!**	我非常高兴
JT:	**See** [you] **Tomorrow!**	**Minngtian jiaan!**	明 天见！

Vocabulary Test = Ccihuii Ceeyaan

INTERNET-ENGLISH	INTERNET-ZHONGWENN	FANGKUAAI HAANZII
Fill in the blanks? = English words	Tiannh koongbbai? Zhongwenn cci	Internet-Zhongwenn Biaanwwei Haanzii □□□□□□□□□□□□
1. ? =	Bbeeijing Faandiaan.	北京饭店.
car	2. ? =	车
count	suaan	算
3. ? =	siji	司机
English	4. ? =	英语
go	zzoou	走
Hello!	Halluo!	哈罗！
5. ? =	duo shhaao	多少
no	6. ? =	不
please	qiinng	请
readying	zhuunnbeei	准备
sir	xiansheng	先生
7. ? =	shuo	说
taxicab	chuzuche	出租车
taximeter	jiijiaaqii	计价器
to	8. ? =	向
9. ? =	huanyinng	欢迎
where	nnaar	哪儿
yes	10. ? =	是的

Scoring and Results

Correct Answers:	1-3 = need practice	4-6 = fair	7-9 = very good	10 = Congratulations!
Duiide Hhuidda:	1-3 = yaao liaanxxi	4-6 = kkeeyyii	7-9 = heenn hhaao	10 = Gongxxii!

田™TiENSTROKES ® USA
www.internetchinese.com * China Certificate of Standardization®1999 * www.tienstrokes.com

TiENSTROKES™

INTERNET-CHINESE™
ALPHABET CHART

1. The Graphic Alphabet

[1] 10 Chinese Graphic Strokes	V•	H•—	L	J	Y	T	G	P	C	Z Z
[2] 10 American Alphabet Names	V-dot	H-stroke	L-stroke	J-stroke	Y-stroke	T-stroke	G-stroke	P-stroke	C-stroke	Z-stroke

2. The Phonic Alphabet Table

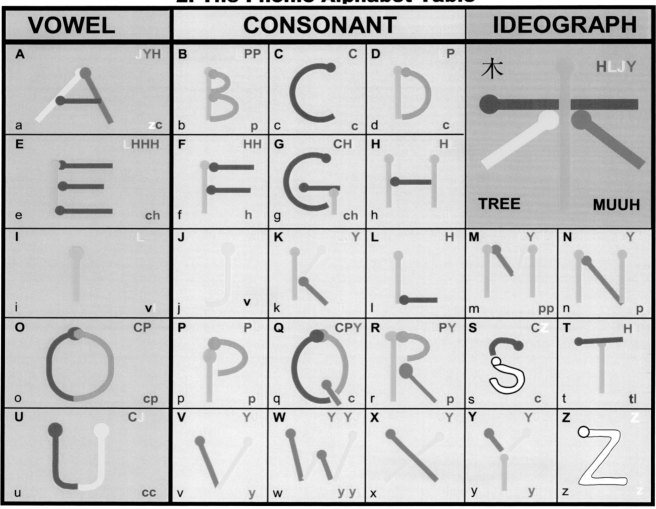

VOWEL		CONSONANT			IDEOGRAPH	
A ... JYH a ... zc		**B** ... PP b ... p	**C** ... C c ... c	**D** ... P d ... c	木 HLJY **TREE** ... **MUUH**	
E ... LHHH e ... ch		**F** ... HH f ... h	**G** ... CH g ... ch	**H** ... H h ... h		
I ... L i ... v		**J** j ... v	**K** ... LY k	**L** ... H l	**M** ... Y m ... pp	**N** ... Y n ... p
O ... CP o ... cp		**P** ... P p ... p	**Q** ... CPY q ... c	**R** ... PY r ... p	**S** ... CZ s ... c	**T** ... H t ... tl
U ... CJ u ... cc		**V** ... Y v ... y	**W** ... YY w ... yy	**X** ... Y x ... x	**Y** ... Y y ... y	**Z** ... Z z ... z

Dr. TiEN says: "Same strokes for all folks!" ™

www.internetchinese.com
Copyright © 1961-2002 by WJP,LLC.
All Rights Reserved

18   USA Patent No. 257,938 ***** China Certificate of Standardization ®1999 ***** PRC Patent No. 88 1 02009.5
Published by Pinxxiee Press -- Printed in the United States of America

10 BASIC LESSONS = 10 JIBEENN KEEWENN = 10 基本 课文

LESSON 1. ALPHABET	KEEVZ 1. ZIIMMUU	课 1 字母		
Table 1: Phonic Letters	Table 2: Pinyin Letters	Table 3: Monosyllabic Characters		
ENGLISH PHONETIC	CHINESE PINYIN	MANDARIN PHONICS		

Vowel	Consonant					Vowel	Consonant					Vowel	Consonant				
A	B	C	D			A	B	C	D			啊 Ah	玻 Bo	雌 Cts	得 De		
E	F	G	H			E	F	G	H			鹅 Ehh	佛 Fo	哥 Geh	喝 He		
I	J	K	L	M	N	I	J	K	L	M	N	衣 yI	基 Ji	科 Ke	勒 Le	摸 Mo	恩 eN
O	P	Q	R	S	T	O	P	Q	R	S	T	喔 wO	坡 Po	欺 cheeQ	日 zz'R	思 Si	特 Te
U	V	W	X	Y	Z	U	V	W	X	Y	Z	呜 wU	维 Vi	我 Wo	希 sheX	丫 Ya	子 Zi

ENGLISH AND CHINESE ALPHABETS COMPARED

The two alphabets, English and Chinese are identical twins, as in [Table 1:] and [Table 2:] above.   If you know one, you recognize the other one, with only 4 letters with different sounds. If you know the English Alphabet, then you know the modern Internet-Chinese Alphabet, automatically. Learn the pronunciation of the Chinese phonics of this twin Alphabet, by studying the above table. The Mandarin phonics are in [Column 3]. Note again: only 4 Chinese Pinyin letters, CRQX, sound somewhat different to the American ear. [Mnemonic: 'CRUX' recalls C R Q X!]. Remember CRQX sound differently in Mandarin, like so: 'C ' = 'ts', 'R' = 'zz'r' , Q = 'chee', and 'X' = 'she'. To get you started, just pronounce Internet-Chinese words like Internet-English as in the 10 basic lessons. To gain confidence, the Internet-Chinese will include an American equivalent pronunciation of the words, e.g. *(shayshay)* as needed, [See Lesson 2. Greetings:]

Thanks.	Xieexiee. *(shayshay)*	谢谢.

There are also 3 more 'retroflexes' of double-consonants: zh; ch; sh. They are pronounced like so: zh as 'j' like in 'jut'; ch as in 'chur'; sh as in 'ssh', respectively. If you know the 26 letters of the Chinese Alphabet sound like English, then you have already learned the basic Pinyin pronunciation of Mandarin, spoken by 85-90% of the Chinese population; and taught 100% in Chinese elementary and middle schools; and used in all high schools and colleges throughout the People's Republic of China. To speak and spell more accurately, you will be happy to know *your* Chinese Language Companion teaches you how to spell the 4 tones, that will enable you to read and spell China's common speech [Ppuutonghuaa], known as Mandarin on TV or Radio.

THE INTERNET-CHINESE METHOD OF SPELLING TONES

In 1969, the author introduced *tone-letters*, akin to the ancient Greeks adding vowel-letters to pure consonant-Hebrew [e.g. Dvd]+ [a, i] to complete syllabic spelling [i.e. David] as in modern English. Before the invention of tone-letters of Internet-Chinese spelling, the 26 phonic letters do not spell the 4 tones of a Mandarin syllable. So, a Tone mark (– , /, V or \ or a number 1, 2, 3 or 4) had to be added. The extra Tone-mark or Tone-number is neither phonetic, nor easy to use. Mandarin words need to be spelled out alphabetically, in order to be naturally readable: e.g. the syllable 'ma' in Mandarin has 4 toned words, which has 4 different meanings: Please compare:

TONES	PINYIN	+TONE-MARK	+TONE-NUMBER	+TONE-LETTER	MEANINGS
1st Tone	ma	mā	ma-1	ma	mother
2nd Tone	ma	má	ma-2	mma	hemp
3rd Tone	ma	mǎ	ma-3	mmaa	horse
4th Tone	ma	mà	ma-4	maa	curse

LESSON 2. GREETINGS	KEEVZ 2. WEENHOOU	课 2. 问候
Internet-English	Internet-Chinese	Chinese Characters
Welcome!	Huanyinng!	欢迎!
How are you?	Nnii hhaao ma?	你 好 吗?
Very well.	Heenn hhaao.	很 好.
Thanks.	Xieexiee. (shayshay)	谢谢.
Good morning.	Nnii zzaao.	你 早.
Good afternoon.	Nnii hhaao.	你 好.
Good-bye.	Zaaijiaan.	再见.
See you tomorrow.	Minngtian jiaan.	明天 见.
See you in a little while.	Hhuittou jiaan.	回头 见.
Yes.	Shiide	是的
No.	Buu shii.	不 是.
All right.	Kkeeyyii.	可以.
Not so.	Buuduii.	不对.
Please.	Qiinng. (chiinng)	请.
Sorry.	Duii buuqqii.	对 不起.
Okay.	Buucuoo. (buu-tsuo)	不错.
What is your surname?	Nnii guii xiingcjh?	你 贵 姓?
My surname is King.	Wwooj xiing Wanng.	我 性 王.
What is your name?	Nnii jiaao shennme minngzii?	你 叫 甚 么 名 字?
My surname is Li.	Wwooj xiingcjh Lliihljy.	我 姓 李.
This is Mrs. King.	Zhee shii Wanng Furenn.	这 是 王 夫人.
This is Mr. Wang.	Zhee shii Wanng Xiansheng (shiansheng).	这 是 王 先生.
This is Miss Wang.	Zhee shii Wanng xxiaaojjiee (shiaaojjiee).	这 是 王 小 姐 .
Pardon me.	Yuannliaang wwooj.	原谅 我.
No problem.	Mmei guanxii (guan-shee).	没 关系.
NOTES	JIILUU	记录

LESSON 3. TRAVELER'S PHRASES	KEEVZ 3. LLEUUXINNG CCIJUU	课 3. 旅行 词句
Internet-English	Internet-Chinese	Chinese Characters
International Travel Service	Gguojii Lleuuxinng Shee	国际 旅行 社
Passport.	Huuzhaao.	护照.
Visa.	Qianzheeng.	签证.
Customs	Hhaaiguan.	海关.
Baggage.	Xinngllii.	行李
Inspection.	Jiaannchha.	检察.
Airplane.	Feiji.	飞机.
Plane ticket.	Feiji Piaao.	飞机 票.
Safety belt.	Anquann-daai.	安全 - 带.
Bathroom.	Ceessuoo.	厕所.
Public Toilet.	Gonggoong Ceessuoo.	公共 厕所.
Ladies.	Nneuu.	女.
Gentlemen.	Nannl	男 .
Toilet Paper.	Weeisheng zhhii.	卫生 纸.
Please wait.	Qiinng deenng yih deenng.	请 等 一 等.
How long?	Duo jjiuuj?	多 久?
I would like to change money.	Wwooj xiaanng huaanqiann.	我 想 换钱 .
Bank.	Yinnhanng.	银行.
I wish you…	Zhuuv ninn…	祝 您…
A safe journey.	Yih Luu Pinng An.	一 路 平 安.
Bon Voyage!	Lleuuxinng Yyukuaai!	愉快!
NOTES	JIILUU	记录

LESSON 4. QUESTIONS & ANSWERS	KEEVZ 4. XUNNWEEN HHE HHUIDDA	课 4. 询问 和 回答
Internet-English	Internet-Chinese	Chinese Characters
Do you understand…	Nnii doonng…	你 懂…
English?	Yingwenn?	英文?
French?	Ffaawenn?	法文?
Japanese?	Riiwenn?	日文?
German?	Ddewenn?	德文?
What?	Shennme?	甚么?
Why?	Weeishennme?	为 甚么?
Where?	Nnaar?	哪儿?
What time (When)?	Shennme shhihoou?	甚么 时候?
Who?	Shhei?	谁?
Which one?	Nnaa yigee?	哪 一个?
How many?	Duo shhaao?	多 少?
How much money?	Duo shhaao qiannjh?	多 少 钱?
How big?	Duo daa?	多 大?
How small?	Duo xxiaao?	多 小?
Do you want?	Yaao buu yaao?	要 不要 ?
Do you have?	Yyoou mmeiyyoou?	有 没有?
Ask or reply.	Ween huoo ddaj.	问 或 答.
I don't understand.	Wwooj buu doonng.	我 不 懂.
I don't want.	Wwooj buu yaao.	我 不 要
I don't have.	Wwooj mmeiyyoou.	我 没有.
I am tired.	Wwooj leeile.	我 累了.
No problem.	Mmei weentti.	没 问题.
I have American dollars.	Wwooj yyoou Mmeeijin.	我 有 美金.
Please help me.	Qiinng bangzhuu wwooj.	请 帮助 我.
Can you?	Kkeeyyii ma?	可以 吗?
NOTES	JIILUU	记录

田™ TiENSTROKES ® USA
www. internetchinese.com * China Certificate of Standardization®1999 * www.tienstrokes.com

LESSON 5. NUMBERS	KEEVZ 5. SHUUZII	课 5. 数字
Internet-English	Internet-Chinese	Chinese Characters
0. zero	0. linng	0. 零
1. one	1. yih	1. 一
2. two	2. eer	2. 二
3. three	3. san	3. 三
4. four	4. sii	4. 四
5. five	5. wwuuh	5. 五
6. six	6. liuuv	6. 六
7. seven	7. qih	7. 七
8. eight	8. ba	8. 八
9. nine	9. jjiuu	9. 九
10. ten	10. shhi	10. 十
11. eleven	11. shhiyih	11. 十一
12. twelve	12. shhieer	12. 十二
13. thirteen	13. shhisan	13. 十三
14. fourteen	14. shhisii	14. 十四
15. fifteen	15. shhiwwuu	15. 十五
16. sixteen	16. shhiliuu	16. 十六
17. seventeen	17. shhiqi	17. 十七
18. eighteen	18. shhiba	18. 十八
19. nineteen	19. shhijjiuu	19. 十九
20. twenty	20. eershhi	20. 二十
21. twenty-one	21. eershhi-yih	21. 二十一
22. twenty-two	22. eershhi-eer	22. 二十二
23. twenty-three	23. eershhi-san	23. 二十三
30. thirty	30. sanshhi	30. 三十
40. forty	40. siishhi	40. 四十
50. fifty	50. wwuushhi	50. 五十
100. one hundred	100. yih bbaai	100. 一百
200. two hundred	200. eer bbaai	200. 二百
1000. one thousand	1000. yih qian	1000. 一千
3000. three thousand	3000. san qian	3000. 三千
10,000. ten-thousand	10,000. yih waan	10,000. 一万
1,000,000. one million	1,000,000. yih bbaaiwaan	1,000,000. 一百万
first, second, third...	diiyih, diieer, diisan...	第一,第二,第三...

⊞™ TiENSTROKES ® USA
www. internetchinese.com * China Certificate of Standardization®1999 * www.tienstrokes.com

LESSON 6. TIME AND DATES	KEEVZ 6. SHHIJIAN HHE RIICHENNG	课6.时间 和 日程
Internet-English	Internet-Chinese	**Chinese Characters**
time (concept)	shhijian (gaainiaan)	时间 (概念)
time (duration)	shhihoou (qijian)	时候 (期间)
wristwatch	shhooubbiaao	手表
clock	zhongjh	钟
o'clock	diaannzhong	点钟
What time is it?	jjii diaannzhong?	几 点钟?
eight o'clock	Ba diaannzhong	八 点钟
two-thirty	liaanng diaann baan	两 点 半
week	xingqi	星期
What day is today?	Jintian xingqi jjii?	今天 星期 几?
Sunday	Xingqirii	星期 日
Monday	Xingqiyih	星期 一
Tuesday	Xingqieer	星期 二
Wednesday	Xingqisan	星期三
Thursday	Xingqisii	星期 四
Friday	Xingqiwwuu	星期 五
Saturday	Xingqiliuu	星期 六
month	yuee	月
January	Yiyuee	一月
February	Eeryuee	二月
March	Sanyuee	三月
April	Siiyuee	四月
May	Wwuuyuee	五月
June	Liuuyuee	六月
July	Qiyuee	七月
August	Bayuee	八月
September	Jjiuuyuee	九月
October	Shhiyuee	十月
November	Shhiyiyuee	十一月
December	Shhieeryuee	十二 月
day	rii	日
year	niann	年
July 4, 1961	1961 Niann Qiyuee 4 Rii	1961 年 7 月 4 日
June 12, 2002	2002 Niann Liuuyuee 12 Rii	2002 年 6 月 12 日

□™ TiENSTROKES ® USA
www. internetchinese.com * China Certificate of Standardization®1999 * www.tienstrokes.com

LESSON 7. MONEY	KEEVZ 7. HUOOBII	课7. 货币
Internet-English	Internet-Chinese	Chinese Characters
money	qiannjh	钱
People's currency	Rennminnbii (Renminbi)	人民币
Yuan	Yuann	元
one yuan	yih yuann	一元
Jiao (10 cents)	Jjiaao (10 fen)	角 (10 分)
two yuan (money)	liaanngkuaai (qiannj)	两块(钱)
Exchange	Duiihuaan	兑换
I would like to…	Wwooj xiaanng…	我想…
to change money.	huaanqiann.	换钱.
Hong Kong dollars.	Gaanngbii.	港币.
cash.	xiaanjin.	现金.
traveler's check.	Lleuuxinng zhipiaao.	旅行 支票.
Credit card.	Xiinyoong kkaapiaan.	信用 卡片.
Where do I sign?	Zaai nnaar qianminng?	在 哪儿 签名?
Please give me…	Qiinng ggeei wwooj…	请给我…
U.S. dollars.	Mmeeijin.	美金.
small change.	linngqiann.	零钱.
Please count it again.	Qiinng zaaii shhuu yixiaa.	请再数 一下.
Correct.	Duiile.	对了.
No matter.	Mmei guanxii.	没 关系.
wallet	ppijiazi	皮夹子
purse	qiannbao	钱包.
NOTES	JIILUU	记录

LESSON 8. FOOD AND DRINKS	KEEVZ 8. SHHIWUU HHE YIINNLIAAO	课 8.食物 和 饮料
Internet-English	Internet-Chinese	Chinese Characters
I'm hungry.	Wwooj eehle.	我 饿 了.
I'm not hungry.	Wwooj buu eeh.	我 不 饿
I'm famished.	Wwooj eeh jjile!	我 饿 极 了!
No more, thanks.	Gooule, xieexiee.	够 了,谢谢.
Dining Room	Canting.	餐厅.
We are…	Wwoomen shii…	我们 是…
The Michigan group.	Mixigen tuann.	密西根 团.
The American group.	Mmeeigguo Tuann.	美国 团.
The Chinese group.	ZhongGguo Tuann	中国 团
Where do we sit?	Wwoomen zuooth zaai nnaar?	我们 坐 在 哪儿?
We'd like to eat…	Wwoomen yaao chi …	我们 要 吃 …
Western food.	Xican.	西餐.
Chinese food***.	Zhongcan.	中餐.
Breakfast.	Zzaaocan.	早餐.
Lunch.	Wwuucan.	午餐.
Dinner.	Waanncan.	晚餐.
I don't take salt.	Wwooj buu chi yannhlt.	我 不 吃 盐.
I would like to drink…	Wwooj yaao he…	我 要 喝 …
coffee.	kafei.	咖啡.
tea.	chha.	茶.
beer.	ppijjiuu.	啤酒.
Coca-Cola.	Kkeekkoou Kkeelee.	可口可乐.
fruit juice.	gguoo zhivvt.	果汁
I would like to order…	Wwooj xiaanng diaann…	我 想 点 …
beef.	nniuroou.	牛肉.
pork.	zhuroou.	猪肉.
chicken	jiroou.	鸡肉
The food was good.	Caai heenn hhaao chi.	菜 很 好 吃.
NOTES	JIILUU	记录
*Hot-&-Sour Soup	Suanlaa Tang	酸辣 汤
*Dumplings	Jjiaaozi	饺子
*Egg roll	Chunjuaann	春卷

田™ TiENSTROKES ® USA
www. internetchinese.com * China Certificate of Standardization®1999 * www.tienstrokes.com

LESSON 9. COMMUNICATIONS	KEEVZ 9. TONGXIIN	课 9. 通信
Internet-English	Internet-Chinese	**Chinese Characters**
Telephone	Diaanhuaa	电话
to telephone.	ddaa diaanhuaa.	打电话.
dial	boh	拨
phone number	diaanhuaa haaommaa	电话号码
What's the number of Mr. Wang?	Wanng Xiansheng de haaommaa shii shennme?	王先生的号码是甚么?
Please write it down.	Qiinng xxiee xiaa llai.	请写下来.
I can't get through.	Ddaa buutong.	打不通.
The line is busy.	Zhaanxiaanle.	占线了.
Whom are you looking for?	Nnii zhhaao shhei?	你找谁?
I'm looking for Miss. Wang.	Wwooj zhhaao Wanng xiaaojjiee.	我找王小姐.
Who are you?	Nnii shii nnaa yi weeiy?	你是哪一位?
I'm sorry, I don't understand.	Duii buu qqii, wwoo ting buu doonng.	对不起, 我听不懂.
One moment please.	Deenng yi xiaa.	等一下.
Please switch me to…	Qiinng zhuaann…	请转…
My phone number is…	Wwoode diaanhuaa haaommaa shii:	我的电话号码是:
Do you speak English?	Nnii shuo Yingwenn ma?	你说英文吗?
Please speak slowly.	Qiinng shuo maanvlv yidiaann.	请说慢一点.
Please speak louder.	Qiinng daasheng yidiaann.	请大声一点.
Wrong number.	Nnii ddaa cuoole.	你打错了.
Please hang up the phone.	Qiinng faang xiaa diaanhuaa.	请放下电话.
Long-distance call.	Channgttu diaanhuaa.	长途电话.
Can you fax?	Nnii nenng chuannzhen ma?	你能传真吗?
Please fax.	Qiinng nnii chuannzhen.	请你传真.
Call me Sunday.	Xingqitian ggeei wwoo ddaa diaanhuaa.	星期天给我打电话.
See (you) again.	Zaaii jiaan.	再见.
May I use your phone?	Wwoo nenng buu nenng yoong yi xiaa ninn de diaanhuaa.	我能不能用一下您的电话.
Please look up Mr. Wang's telephone number.	Qiinng bangzhuu wwoo chhazhhaao Wanng Xiansheng diaanhuaa.	请帮助我查找王先生电话.

LESSON 10. CHINESE GRAPHIC ALPHABET	KEEVZ 10. ZHONGWENN XIAANGXINNG ZIIMMUU	课 10. 中文 象形 字母
Internet-English	Internet-Chinese	Chinese Characters
The 10 TiENSTROKES letters can spell-write English & Chinese Characters	Zhee 10 SHHiBBIiHUAA Ziittii nenng pinxxiee Yingwenn & Haanzii	这 10 十笔画字体 能 拼写 英文 & 汉字

If you also wish to learn to recognize square Chinese Characters, then you need to learn the Tenstrokes Alphabet (TiENSTROKES). It is relatively easy by using 10 English letters to decode all the inscrutable Chinese characters. This TiENSTROKES key can decode all 60, 000+ Chinese ideographs with the 10 graphic strokes. The 10 graphic strokes can also write the 26 English letters as 26 Chinese characters. The following table is easy grasp, to use and also fun to learn and master this new idea.

[1] TiENSTROKES CHINESE GRAPHIC ALPHABET EXERCISE

STROKE #	Step i: Learn 10 English Letter Names and give to the 10 basic Chinese strokes in the next column:	Step ii. Trace and copy the 10 Chinese Strokes to learn how characters are made:	Step iii: Pair 10 English letters with the TiENSTROKES graphic strokes:	Step iv: Say the 10 English Letters aloud but copy the 10 graphic strokes, as in the next column, until you know the English names and remember the 10 Chinese strokes:	Step v. Write the TiENSTROKES Global Alphabet strokes from memory, just for fun, like so:
0	V dot-stroke	、	V 、	V-dot	、
1	H stroke	一	H 一	H-stroke	一
2	L stroke	丨	L 丨	L-stroke	丨
3	J stroke	丿	J 丿	J-stroke	丿
4	Y stroke	丶	Y 丶	Y-stroke	丶
5	T stroke	⼀	T ⼀	T-stroke	⼀
6	G stroke	乚	G 乚	G-stroke	乚
7	P stroke	乛	P 乛	P-stroke	乛
8	C stroke	∟	C ∟	C-stroke	∟
9	Z stroke	乙	Z 乙	Z-stroke	乙

NOW TRY THE 2 EXERCISES, [A] and [B]:

English Exercise [A]: Say 'J stroke, Y stroke, H stroke' ,
but write strokes like so: ' 丿 一 丶 '=> **'A'**
Note: any English letters can be written with TiENSTROKES.

Chinese Exercise [B]: Say 'H stroke, L-stroke, J stroke Y stroke'
but write strokes like so: ' 一 丨 丿 丶 '=> '木'
Note: any Chinese characters can also be written with TiENSTROKES.

Now, you are writing both *phonic letters* and *graphic characters* with the same strokes of Global Alphabet. Note: Master [1] the TiENSTROKES Chinese Alphabet; [2] the Global Alphabet Chart how to decode; [3] how to decode any Chinese ideograph with the same 10 StrokeLetters; [4] to use Internet-Chinese ⇔ Internet-English Dictionary (see Introduction to Internet-Chinese ⇔ Internet-English Script). You can practice TiENSTROKES by playing 3 SPELLCHECKER GAMES:

SPELL-CHECKER GAME#1
TiENSTROKES ⇔ IDEOGRAPHS ⇔ ENGLISH

TiENSTROKES 田氏 十笔画 TIANNSHII SHHIBIHUA	IDEOGRAM 汉字 HAANZII	*ENGLISH* 英文 *YINGWENN*	INTERNET-CHINESE 因特网 中文 YINTEWANG ZHONGWENN
A a			
B b			
C c			
C	乚	C-stroke	C-bbiihuaa
CHL	G	G	G
CJ	U	U	U
CJH	女	female	nneuu
CP	O	O	O
CPY	Q	Q	Q
VCVV	心	heart	xin
CZ	S	S	S
D d			
E e			
F f			
G g			
G	ι	G-stroke	G-bbiihuaa
GVJV	以	use	yyii
H h			
H	一	H-stroke	H-bbiihuaa
H	一	one	yih
HC	七	seven	qi
HCHL	车	car	che
HCJC	比	compare	bbii
HCJY	区	ou-name	ou
HGJV	戈	spear	gexvx
HH	二	two	eer
HHH	三	three	san
HHJ	于	at	yyuh

TiENSTROKES 田氏 十笔画 TIANNSHII SHHIBIHUA	IDEOGRAM 汉字 HAANZII	*ENGLISH* 英文 *YINGWENN*	INTERNET-CHINESE 因特网 中文 YINTEWANG ZHONGWENN
HHJVV	示	show	shiihh
HHJY	夫	fellow	fu
HHJY	天	heaven	tian
HHL	干	do	gaan
HHLH	王	king	wanng
HJHLH	左	left-side	zzuooh
HJLPH	右	right-side	yoouh
HJLV	不	not	buu
HJP	万	10,000	waan
HJPY	友	friend	yyoouhx
HJTHJ	打	hit	ddaa
HJY	大	big	daa
HL	十	ten	shhi
HLH	工	work	gongh
HLHCV	去	go	quu
HLHX	土	soil	ttuu
HLJY	木	tree	muuh
HLJYH	本	root	beenn
HLLHH	耳	ear	eerr
HLPH	五	five	wwuuh
HLPHJ	可	able	kkee
HLV	下	down	xiaa
I i			
J j			
J	丿	J-stroke	J-bbiihuaa
JCV	么	what	me
JHHJ	手	hand	shhoouj
JHHLH	生	grow	sheng
JHHZ	气	air	qii

TiENSTROKES 田氏 十笔画 TIANNSHII SHHIBIHUA	IDEOGRAM 汉字 HAANZII	*ENGLISH* 英文 *YINGWENN*	INTERNET-CHINESE 因特网 中文 YINTEWANG ZHONGWENN
JJHLPH	后	after	hoou
JJV	小	little	xxiaao
JLHL	什	what's	shenn
JLPHH	白	white	bbai
JLPLC	他	he	ta
JLVLP	们	plural	men
JP	力	power	lii
JPHH	月	moon	yuee
JPJY	水	water	shhuii
JPLPH	加	add	jia
JPVZH	鸟	bird	nniaao
JV	八	eight	ba
JVJY	从	follow	conng
JVPJ	分	cent	fen
JY	人	person	renn
JYH	A	a	a
JYHHCV	会	meet	huii
JYL	个	unit	gee
JYVP	今	today	jinv
JZ	几	how-many	jjii
JZJY	风	wind	feng
JZX	九	nine	jjiuu
K k			
L l			
L	丨	L-stroke	L-bbiihuaa
LCL	山	hill	shan
LH	L	L	L
LHH	F	F	F
LHH	上	up	shaang
LHHH	E	E	E
LHLH	止	stop	zhhii
LJVJ	少	few	shhaao
LJY	K	k	k
LLH	H	h	h

TiENSTROKES 田氏 十笔画 TIANNSHII SHHIBIHUA	IDEOGRAM 汉字 HAANZII	*ENGLISH* 英文 *YINGWENN*	INTERNET-CHINESE 因特网 中文 YINTEWANG ZHONGWENN
LLVJH	业	job	yee
LP	D	D	d
LPH	口	mouth	kkoou
LPHH	日	sun	rii
LPHHC	电	electric	diaan
LPHHH	目	eye	muu
LPHHT	旦	dawn	daan
LPHJHZ	吃	eat	chi
LPHL	中	middle	zhong
LPHLH	田	fields	tiann
LPHLHV	虫	crawler	chonng
LPJC	见	see	jiaan
LPJCH	四	four	sii
LPP	B	b	b
LPY	R	r	R
LYJL	M	m	m
LYL	N	n	n
M m			
N n			
O o			
P p			
P	丁	P-stroke	P-bbiihuaa
PHGHG	民	people	minn
PHZ	弓	bow	gongp
PJ	刀	knife	dao
PJ	了	-ed [verb]	-le [doongcci]
PJH	子	seed	zzii
PJLPY	皮	skin	ppi
PL	P	p	p
PLC	也	also	yyee
PY	又	again	yoou
PYHJV	对	correct	duii
PZH	马	horse	mmaa
Q q			
R r			

TiENSTROKES 田氏 十笔画 TIANNSHII SHHIBIHUA	IDEOGRAM 汉字 HAANZII	ENGLISH 英文 YINGWENN	INTERNET-CHINESE 因特网 中文 YINTEWANG ZHONGWENN
S s			
T t			
T	⺄	T-stroke	T-bbiihuaa
U u			
V v			
V	丶	V-stroke	V-bbiihuaa
VHJP	方	square	fang
VHJV	六	six	liuu
VHPJ	方	square	fang
VJJY	火	fire	hhuoo
VJPV	为	for	weei
VLP	门	door	menn

TiENSTROKES 田氏 十笔画 TIANNSHII SHHIBIHUA	IDEOGRAM 汉字 HAANZII	ENGLISH 英文 YINGWENN	INTERNET-CHINESE 因特网 中文 YINTEWANG ZHONGWENN
VPY	之	's	zhi
VVHJY	头	head	ttou
VVPCJH	安	peace	an
W w			
X x			
Y y			
YJ	入	enter	ruu
YJL	Y	Y	Y
YJYJ	W	W	W
Z z			
Z	乙	Z-stroke	Z-bbiihuaa

SPELL-CHECKER GAME# 2
ENGLISH ⇔ IDEOGRAPHS ⇔ TiENSTROKES

ENGLISH 英文 YINGWENN	IDEOGRAM 汉字 HAANZII	TiENSTROKES 田氏十笔画 TIANNSHII SHHIBIHUA	INTERNET-CHINESE 因特网 中文 YINTEWANG ZHONGWENN
A a			
a	A	JYH	a
able	可	HLPHJ	kkee
add	加	JPLPH	jia
after	后	JJHLPH	Hoou
again	又	PY	yoou
air	气	JHHZ	qii
also	也	PLC	yyee
at	于	HHJ	yyuh
B b			
b	B	LPP	b
big	大	HJY	daa
bird	鸟	JPVZH	nniaao
bow	弓	PHZ	gongp
C c			
c	C	C	c
car	车	HCHL	che
cent	分	JVPJ	fen
compare	比	HCJC	bbii
correct	对	PYHJV	duii
crawler	虫	LPHLHV	chonng
D d			
d	D	LP	d
dawn	旦	LPHHT	daan
do	干	HHL	gaan
door	门	VLP	menn
down	下	HLV	xiaa
E e			
e	E	LHHH	e
ear	耳	HLLHH	eerr
eat	吃	LPHJHZ	chi
-ed [verb]	了	PJ	-le [doongcci]

ENGLISH 英文 YINGWENN	IDEOGRAM 汉字 HAANZII	TiENSTROKES 田氏十笔画 TIANNSHII SHHIBIHUA	INTERNET-CHINESE 因特网 中文 YINTEWANG ZHONGWENN
eight	八	JV	ba
electric	电	LPHHC	diaan
enter	入	YJ	ruu
eye	目	LPHHH	muu
F f			
f	F	LHH	f
fellow	夫	HHJY	fu
female	女	CJH	nneuu
few	少	LJVJ	shhaao
fields	田	LPHLH	tiann
fire	火	VJJY	hhuoo
five	五	HLPH	wwuuh
follow	从	JVJY	conng
for	为	VJPV	weei
four	四	LPJCH	sii
friend	友	HJPY	yyoouhx
G g			
G	G	CHL	G
go	去	HLHCV	quu
grow	生	JHHLH	sheng
H h			
h	H	LLH	h
hand	手	JHHJ	shhoouj
he	他	JLPLC	ta
head	头	VVHJY	ttou
heart	心	VCVV	xin
heaven	天	HHJY	tian
hill	山	LCL	shan
hit	打	HJTHJ	ddaa
horse	马	PZH	mmaa
how-many	几	JZ	jjii

ENGLISH 英文 YINGWENN	IDEOGRAM 汉字 HAANZII	TiENSTROKES 田氏十笔画 TIANNSHII SHHIBIHUA	INTERNET-CHINESE 因特网 中文 YINTEWANG ZHONGWENN
I i			
Into	入	YJ	ruu
J j			
J	J	HJ	J
job	业	LLVJH	yee
K k			
k	K	LJY	k
king	王	HHLH	wanng
knife	刀	PJ	dao
L l			
L	L	LH	L
left-side	左	HJHLH	zzuooh
little	小	JJV	xxiaao
M m			
m	M	LYJL	m
meet	会	JYHHCV	huii
middle	中	LPHL	zhong
moon	月	JPHH	yuee
mouth	口	LPH	kkoou
N n			
n	N	LYL	n
nine	九	ZJ	jjiuu
not	不	HJLV	buu
O o			
O	O	CP	O
of	之	VPY	zhi
one	一	H	yih
Ou-name	区	HCJY	ou
P p			
p	P	PL	p
peace	安	VVPCJH	an
people	民	PHGHG	minn
person	人	JY	renn
plural	们	JLVLP	menjl

ENGLISH 英文 YINGWENN	IDEOGRAM 汉字 HAANZII	TiENSTROKES 田氏十笔画 TIANNSHII SHHIBIHUA	INTERNET-CHINESE 因特网 中文 YINTEWANG ZHONGWENN
power	力	JP	lii
Q q			
Q	Q	CPY	Q
R r			
r	R	LPY	R
right-side	右	HJLPH	Yoouh
root	本	HLJYH	beenn
S s			
S	S	CZ	S
see	见	LPJC	jiaan
seed	子	PJH	zzii
seven	七	HC	qi
show	示	HHJVV	shiihh
six	六	VHJV	liuu
skin	皮	PJLPY	ppi
soil	土	HLHX	ttuu
spear	戈	HGJV	gexvx
square	方	VHJP	fang
square	方	VHPJ	fang
stop	止	LHLH	zhhii
sun	日	LPHH	rii
T t			
T	T	TL	T
ten	十	HL	shhi
ten thousand	万	HJP	waan
three	三	HHH	san
today	今	JYVP	jinv
tree	木	HLJY	muuhljy
two	二	HH	eer
U u			
u	U	CJ	u
unit	个	JYL	gee

ENGLISH 英文 YINGWENN	IDEOGRAM 汉字 HAANZII	TiENSTROKES 田氏十笔画 TIANNSHII SHHIBIHUA	INTERNET-CHINESE 因特网 中文 YINTEWANG ZHONGWENN
up	上	LHH	shaang
use	以	GVJV	yyii
V v			
v	V	V	v
W w			
w	W	YJYJ	w
water	水	JPJY	shhuii
what	么	JCV	me
what's	什	JLHL	shenn

ENGLISH 英文 YINGWENN	IDEOGRAM 汉字 HAANZII	TiENSTROKES 田氏十笔画 TIANNSHII SHHIBIHUA	INTERNET-CHINESE 因特网 中文 YINTEWANG ZHONGWENN
white	白	JLPHH	bbai
wind	风	JZJY	feng
work	工	HLH	gongh
X x			
x	X	YT	x
Y y			
y	Y	YJL	y
Z z			
z	Z	Z	z

SPELL-CHECKER GAME#3
INTERNET-CHINESE ⇔ IDEOGRAPHS ⇔ TiENSTROKES

INTERNET-CHINESE 因特网 中文 YINTEWANG ZHONGWENN	IDEOGRAM 汉字 HAANZII	TiENSTROKES 田氏十笔画 TIANNSHII SHHIBIHUA	ENGLISH 英文 YINGWENN
A a			
a	A	JYH	a
an	安	VVPCJH	peace
B b			
b	B	LPP	b
ba	八	JV	eight
bbai	白	JLPHH	white
bbii	比	HCJC	compare
beenn	本	HLJYH	root
buu	不	HJLV	not
C c			
C-bbiihuaa	L	C	C-stroke
che	车	HCHL	car
chi	吃	LPHJHZ	eat
chonng	虫	LPHLHV	crawler
conng	从	JVJY	follow
D d			
d	D	LP	D
daa	大	HJY	big
daan	旦	LPHHT	dawn
dao	刀	PJ	knife
ddaa	打	HJTHJ	hit
diaan	电	LPHHC	electric
duii	对	PYHJV	correct
E e			
e	E	LHHH	e
eer	二	HH	two
eerr	耳	HLLHH	ear
F f			
f	F	LHH	F
fang	方	VHJP	square

INTERNET-CHINESE 因特网 中文 YINTEWANG ZHONGWENN	IDEOGRAM 汉字 HAANZII	TiENSTROKES 田氏十笔画 TIANNSHII SHHIBIHUA	ENGLISH 英文 YINGWENN
fang	方	VHPJ	square
fen	分	JVPJ	cent
feng	风	JZJY	wind
fu	夫	HHJY	fellow
G g			
G-bbiihuaa	L	G	G-stroke
gaan	干	HHL	do
gee	个	JYL	unit
gexvx	戈	HGJV	spear
gongh	工	HLH	work
gongp	弓	PHZ	bow
H h			
H-bbiihuaa	一	H	H-stroke
hhuoo	火	VJJY	fire
hoou	后	JJHLPH	after
huii	会	JYHHCV	meet
J j			
J-bbiihuaa	丿	J	J-stroke
jia	加	JPLPH	add
jiaan	见	LPJC	see
jinv	今	JYVP	today
jjii	几	JZ	how-many
jjiuu	九	JZX	nine
K k			
k	K	LJY	k
kkee	可	HLPHJ	able
kkoou	口	LPH	mouth
L l			
L-bbiihuaa	丨	L	L-stroke
le [guooquu/doongcci]	了	PJ	ed [past/verb]

INTERNET-CHINESE 因特网 中文 YINTEWANG ZHONGWENN	IDEOGRAM 汉字 HAANZII	TiENSTROKES 田氏十笔画 TIANNSHII SHHIBIHUA	ENGLISH 英文 YINGWENN
lii	力	JP	power
liuu	六	VHJV	six
M m			
m	M	LYJL	m
me	么	JCV	what
menn	门	VLP	door
menjl	们	JLVLP	plural
minn	民	PHGHG	people
mmaa	马	PZH	horse
muu	目	LPHHH	eye
muuhljy	木	HLJY	tree
N n			
n	N	LYL	n
nneuu	女	CJH	female
nniaao	鸟	JPVZH	bird
O o			
O	O	CP	O
ou	区	HCJY	Ou-name
P p			
P-bbiihuaa	乛	P	P-stroke
ppi	皮	PJLPY	skin
Q q			
Q	Q	CPY	Q
qi	七	HC	seven
qii	气	JHHZ	air
quu	去	HLHCV	go
R r			
R	R	LPY	R
renn	人	JY	person
rii	日	LPHH	sun
ruu	入	YJ	enter
S s			
s	S	CZ	s
san	三	HHH	three
shaang	上	LHH	up

INTERNET-CHINESE 因特网 中文 YINTEWANG ZHONGWENN	IDEOGRAM 汉字 HAANZII	TiENSTROKES 田氏十笔画 TIANNSHII SHHIBIHUA	ENGLISH 英文 YINGWENN
shan	山	LCL	hill
sheng	生	JHHLH	grow
shenn	什	JLHL	what's
shhaao	少	LJVJ	few
shhi	十	HL	ten
shhoouj	手	JHHJ	hand
shhuii	水	JPJY	water
shiihh	示	HHJVV	show
sii	四	LPJCH	four
T t			
T-bbiihuaa	一	T	T-stroke
tay	他	JLPLC	he
tian	天	HHJY	heaven
tiann	田	LPHLH	fields
ttou	头	VVHJY	head
ttuu	土	HLHX	soil
U u			
U	U	CJ	U
V v			
V-bbiihuaa	、	V	V-stroke
W w			
W	W	YJYJ	W
waan	万	HJP	ten thousand
wanng	王	HHLH	king
weei	为	VJPV	for
wwuuh	五	HLPH	five
X x			
X	X	YT	X
xiaa	下	HLV	down
xin	心	VCVV	heart
xxiaao	小	JJV	little
Y y			
Y-bbiihuaa	＼	Y	Y-stroke
yee	业	LLVJH	job

INTERNET-CHINESE 因特网 中文 YINTEWANG ZHONGWENN	IDEOGRAM 汉字 HAANZII	TiENSTROKES 田氏十笔画 TIANNSHII SHHIBIHUA	ENGLISH 英文 YINGWENN
yih	一	H	one
yoou	又	PY	again
Yoouh	右	HJLPH	right-side
yuee	月	JPHH	moon
yyee	也	PLC	also
yyii	以	GVJV	use
yyoouhx	友	HJPY	friend
yyuh	于	HHJ	at

INTERNET-CHINESE 因特网 中文 YINTEWANG ZHONGWENN	IDEOGRAM 汉字 HAANZII	TiENSTROKES 田氏十笔画 TIANNSHII SHHIBIHUA	ENGLISH 英文 YINGWENN
Z z			
Z-bbiihuaa	乙	Z	Z-stroke
zhhii	止	LHLH	stop
zhi	之	VPY	of
zhong	中	LPHL	middle
zzii	子	PJH	seed
zzuooh	左	HJHLH	left-side

CHINESE 'BIRD WATCHING' GAME

No knowledge of-Chinese required.

Are you ready to play a NEW game? Good.
We look upon each inscrutable Chinese Character,
for an example: '鸟' as a 'BIRD'!

After spotting a bird like this one '鸟', observe its features, i.e. its strokes,
JPVZH, then decode and identify this character '鸟' in English as BIRD!
Do it on your own or in competition with your friends. That's the game.
You can identify any of the thousands of Chinese characters, such as
鸟,十,三,木..., flying around us anywhere in the world!

Only requirement is the bilingual 'Binoculars', as below! TiENSTROKES Alphameric Code:

0	1	2	3	4	5	6	7	8	9
丶 = V	一 = H	丨 = L	丿 = J	丶 = Y	一 = T	乚 = G	乛 = P	乚 = C	乙 = Z

FOUR (4) STEPS OF THE GAME

STEP 1: SPOT a Bird'	STEP 2: DECODE its strokes	STEP 3: IMITATE its 'call'	STEP 4: READ its meaning
"BIRDS" = Characters	Into TIENSTROKES Letters	In Mandarin-CHINESE	In American-ENGLISH
三 ⇔ 一 一 一	HHH ⇔ 三	san	three
十 ⇔ 一 丨	HL ⇔ 十	shhi	ten
木 ⇔ 一 丨 丿 丶	HLJY ⇔ 木	muuh	tree
鸟 ⇔ 丿 乛 丶 乙 一	JPVZH ⇔ 鸟	nniaao	bird
Help 1:	*Help 2:*	*Help 3:*	*Help 4:*

Help 1	Help 2	Help 3	Help 4
Spot Chinese Characters as our 'Birds'. Then, observe and identify Its Strokes. Take the strokes apart in your mind or on paper. Count the strokes. Then order the strokes in natural sequence, from left to right; top to bottom. Ready for converting the strokes to the TiENSTROKES letters!	Decode & Convert each graphic Chinese brush stroke within the square character into one of the TiENSTROKES Letters: that is, each graphic stroke is assigned a unique phonic letter: 丶 ⇔ V 一 ⇔ H 丨 ⇔ L 丿 ⇔ J 丶 ⇔ Y 一 ⇔ T 乚 ⇔ G 乛 ⇔ P 乚 ⇔ C 乙 ⇔ Z The rule of stroke-order in decoding is to decode from a square format to a linear format, that is, from the left to right, then top to bottom, stroke by stroke, accordingly. Use the TiENSTROKES CODE. [See sample "Birds" below]	Sound out the Internet-Chinese Mandarin word. An Internet-Chinese spelling is 1:1 equivalent of a Chinese character. It is composed of **Pinyin+Toneletter + 1st Strokeletter** or more if necessary to be the exact corresponding character.	Learn the <u>meaning</u> in ENGLISH. Can you decode 3 out of the 4 "Birds" '三"十"木"目 correctly? If you do, You <u>have got it!</u> Reward: After recognizing 100 "Birds" or so, you will have a golden key to Chinese culture. *Practice makes perfect.*

You will be seeing such 'Birds' or 'Chinese characters' on the Web,
on a lunch menu in a Chinese Restaurant, or on storefronts in Chinatowns.
Following is a list of commonly used characters in the Streets in Beijing,
Shanghai, Hong Kong or Taiwan.
When you spot them, you will have fun in decoding them according to
the following trilingual table,
a Traveler's Guide to "Chinese Birds, *Real Characters!*":
You can practice your
'BIRD-WATCHING' skill by playing with the following "BIRDS" list:

"BIRDS"	In TiENSTROKES CODE ALPHABETIC ORDER	Internet-Chinese	Internet-English
	ABC		
▯女	CJH 女▯▯	Nneuu	Female
▯女 (厕所)	CJH 女 (HJ-LP-JV-LJ厕▯▯JJPH-JHL所▯▯▯▯	Nneuu (Ceessuoo)	Ladies (Toilet)
收	CL-JHJY 收	Shou	Receive
收款处	CL-JHJY收 HLH-HH-JJV-JPJY 款 JPY-LV 处	Shoukuaan Chuu	Cashier
出	CLL-CL出	Chu	Exit
出租车	CLL-CL出 JHLV-LPHHH租 HCHL▯车	Chuzu Che	Taxi Cab
出口	CLL-CL出 LPH口	Chukkoou	Exit
	DE F G H		
一	H 一	Yih	One
一号	H 一 LPH-HZ号	Yih Haao	One #
一号 站台	H 一 LPH-HZ号 VH-VJT-LH-LPH站 CV-LPH台	Yih Haao Zhaanttai	1 # Platform
牙医	HCJJ牙 H-JH-HJV-C医	Yyayih	Dentists
软席	HCLT-JPJY 软 VHJ-HLLH-LPL席	Ruaannxxi	Soft Seat
成人 票	HCP-GJV成 JY人 H-LP-LLH-HH-JJV▯票	Chenngrenn Piaao	Adult Tickets
开门	HHJL开 VLP门	Kaimenn	Open(Door)

"BIRDS"	In TiENSTROKES CODE ALPHABETIC ORDER	Internet-Chinese	Internet-English
有人	HJ- LPHH有 JY人	Yyoou-Renn	Occupied/ Person
医生	H-JH-HJV-C医 J-HHLH生	Yishengh	Doctors
医院	H-JH-HJV-C医 ZL-VV-HHJC院	Yiyuaan	Hospital
左	HJ-HLH左	Zzuoo	Left-Side
硬席	HJ-LPH-HLPHH-JY硬 VHJ-HLLH-LPL席	Yiingxxi	Hard Seat
右	HJ-LPH右	Yoouh	Right[Side]
厕所	HJ-LP-JV-LJ厕 JJPH-JJHL所	Ceessuoo	Toilets
不准 超车	HJLV不 VT-JL-V-HHHLH准 HLH-LHJY- PJ- LPH超 HCHL车	Buuzhuunn Chaoche	No Passing
不准 停 车	HJLV不 VTJL-V-HHHLH准 JL-VH-LPH-VP-HJ停 HCHL车	Buuzhuunn Tinng Che	No Parking
抵达/ 到达	HJT-JGHGV抵 HJV-VZY达/ HCV- HLT- LJ到 HJV-VZY达	Ddiidda/ Daaodda	Arrivals
推/拉	HJT-JL- V-HHHLH推 / HJT-VHVJH拉	Tui/La	Push/Pull
热水	HJT-JZV-VVVV热 JPJY水	Ree Shhuii	Hot Water
接待处	HJT-VHVJH-CJH接 JJL-HLH-HJV待 JPY-LV处	Jiedaaichuu	Reception Area
博物馆	HL-HLP-HHLV-HJV博 JHLT-JPJJ物 JPG-VVP-LPHPH馆	Bbowuuguaann [Bowuguan]	Relics Hall [Museum]
禁止	HLJV-HLJY-HH-JJV禁 LHLH止	Jiinzhhii	Prohibit
禁止 牌 照	HLJV-HLJY-HH-JJV禁 LHLH止 JLHP-JLPHHJ H L牌 LPHH-PJLPH- VVVV照	Jiinzhhii Ppaizhaao	Prohibit Photography
禁止 吸烟	HLJV-HLJY-HH-JJV禁 LHLH止 LPH- JZY吸 VJJV-LP-HJV-H烟	Jiinzhhii Xiyan	Prohibit Smoking

⊞ ™ TiENSTROKES ® USA
www. internetchinese.com * China Certificate of Standardization®1999 * www.tienstrokes.com

"BIRDS"	In TiENSTROKES CODE ALPHABETIC ORDER	Internet-Chinese	Internet-English
禁止 游泳	HLJV-HLJY-HH-JJV禁 LHLH止 VVT-VHPJ-JH-PJH游 VVT-VJPJY泳	Jiinzhhii Yyouyoonng	Prohibit Swimming
警 告	HLL-JP-LPH-JHJY-VH-HH-LPH警 JHLH-LPH告	Jiinngaao	Warning
警察	HLL-JP-LPH-JHJY-VH-HH-LPH警 VVP-JPV-YP-HHJJV察	Jiinngchha	Police
茶 点	HLL-JY-HJJV茶 LH LPH-VVVV点	Chhadiaan	Refreshments
地下 通道	HLT-PLC 地 HLV下 PV-LPHHL-VZY通 VJH-JLPHHHVZY道	Diixiaa Tongddaao	Underpass Subway
地下室	HLT-PLC 地 HLV下 VVP- HCV- HLH室	Diixiaashi	Basement
地铁	HLT-PLC地 JHHHG-JHHJY铁	Diittiee	Subway Train
	I J		
停 靠处	J- VH-LPH-VP-HJ停 JHL- LPH-LHHH LHHH靠 JPY V处	Tinngkaao Chuu	Parking Stand
儿童 票	JC儿 VHVJH- LPHH-HLH童 HLPLLH-HHJJV票	Errtonng Piaao	Children Tickets
饮用 水	JHG-JPJY饮 JPHHL用 JPJY水	Yiinnyoong Shhuii	Drinking Water
长辈 票	JHGY长 LHHH-LHHH- HCHL辈 HLPLLH-HHJJV票	Zhaanngbeei Piaao	Senior Tickets
银行	JHHHG-PHHGJY银 JJL-HHJ行	Yinnhanng	Bank
失物 处	JHHJY失 JHT-JPJJ物 JPY LV处	Shiwuu Chhuu	Lost-And-Found
午休	JHHL午 JL-HLJY休	Wwuuxiu	Noon Rest
靠左 行驶	JHH-LPH-LHHH-LHHH靠 HJ-HLH左 JJL-HHJ行 PZT-LPHJY驶	Kaao Zuoohj Xinngshhii	Keep Left To Travel

"BIRDS"	In TiENSTROKES CODE ALPHABETIC ORDER	Internet-Chinese	Internet-English
靠右行驶	JHH-LPH-LHHH-LHHH靠 HJ-HLH右 JJL-HHJ行 PZT-LPHJY驶	Kaao Yoouhj Xinngshhii	Keep Right To Travel
行李认领	JJL- HHJ行 HLJY-PJH李 VZ-JY认 JVVPV-HJ-LPJV领	Xinngllii Reenliinng	Baggage Claim
小心	JJV小 VCVV心	Xxiaaoxin	Caution
小心台阶	JJV小 VCVV心 CV-LPH台 ZL-JYJL阶	Xxiaaoxin Ttaijie	Caution Steps
保留座位	JL-LPH-HLJY保 JCV- PJ-LPHLH留 VHJ-JV-JV-HLH座 JL-VHVJH位	Bbaaolliu Zuooweei	Reserved Seats
停	JL-VH- LPH- V-HJ停	Tinng	Stop
自动扶梯	JLP-HHH自 HHCV-JP 动 HJT-HHJY扶 HLJV-VJPHZ-LJ梯	Ziidoong Ffuti	Escalator
危险	JP-HJ PC危 ZL-JY-JVVJH险	Weixiaann	Danger
免税店	JP-LPH-JC免 JHLJV-VJ-LPH-JC税 VHJ-LH-LPH店	Miaannshuii Diaanvhj	Duty Free Shop
免费入内	JP-LPH-JC 免 PHZ-JL- LPJV费 YJ入 LPJV内	Miaannfeei Ruuneei	Free Admission
边防检察	JP VZY边 ZL-VHJP防 HLJV- JY-HVVJH检 VVP-JPV-VYP-HH-JJV察	Bianfanng Jiaannchha	Border Control
入口	JY入 LPH口	Ruukkoou	Enter
公共汽车	JY-CV公 HLLH-JV共 VVT-HJJZ汽 HCHL车	Gonggoong Qiiche	Public Bus
公共浴室	JY-CV公 HLLH-JV共 VVT-JV-JY-LPH浴 VVP-HCV-HLH室	Gonggoong Yuus Shiivm	Public Bath
	K L		
止步	LHLH止 LHLH-LJJ步	Zhhiibuu	Halt

⊞™ TiENSTROKES ® USA
www.internetchinese.com * China Certificate of Standardization®1999 * www.tienstrokes.com

"BIRDS"	In TiENSTROKES CODE ALPHABETIC ORDER	Internet-Chinese	Internet-English
紧急 出口	LL-PY-CCV-JJV紧 JP-PHH-VCVV急 CLL-CL出 LPH口	Jiinnjji Chukkoou	Emergency Exit
男	LPHH-JP男	Nannl	Men (Toilets)
晚点	LPHH-JPLPH-JC晚 LH-LPH-VVVV点	Waanndiaann	Delayed
电梯	LPHHC电 HLJV-VJ -PHZ LJ梯	Diaantti	Elevator
邮局	LPHHL-ZL 邮 PHJ-P-LPH局	Yyoujju	Post Office
	M N O P		
通 行费	PV-LPHHL-VZY通 JJL-HHJ行 PHZ-JL-LPJV费	Tongxinng Feei	Toll Fee
登	PV-YJJ-H-LPH-VJH登	Deng	Ascend
登机 门	PV-YJJ-H-LPH-V J H 登 HLJV-JZ机 VLP门	Dengjimenn	Airline Gate
	Q R S T U V		
衣 帽 室	VH-JGJY衣 LPL-LPHH-LPHHH 帽 VVP-HCV-HLH室	Yimaao Shiivvp	Coat Room
交叉 口	VH-JVJY交 PYV叉 LPH口	Jiaochakkoou	Junction Point
交通 灯	VH-JVJY交 PV-LPHHL-VZY通 VJJV-HJ灯	Jiaotong Deng	Traffic Lights
离 境/ 发 车	VH-JY-CL-LP-CV离 HLT-VHVJH-LPHH-JC境/ CJ-PY-V发 HCHL 车	Llijiing/Fache	Departures/ Vehicles
高 速公 路	VH-LPH-LP-LPH高 HLPH-JJV-VZY速 JY-CV公 LPH-LHLT-JPY-JPH路	Gaosuu Gongluu	Super Highway
市 府政 大楼	VH-LPL市 HLHLT-JHJY政 VHJ-JLHJG政 HLY大 HLJV-VJ-HLJY-CJH楼	Shiivh Zheengffuu Daallou	City (Government) Hall
部	VHVJH-LPH-ZL部	Buuv.	Depart.

"BIRDS"	In TiENSTROKES CODE ALPHABETIC ORDER	Internet-Chinese	Internet-English
关门	VJ HHJY关　VLP门	Guan Menn	Closed Door
火车	VJJY火　HCHL车	Hhuooche	Train
问讯 处	VLP- LPH问　VZ -ZHL讯 JPY-LV处	Weenxuun Chuu	Inquiry Desk
闲人 没入	VLP-HLJY闲　JY人 VVT-JZ PY囗没　YJ入	Xiannrenn Mooruu	No Trespasser
减价 出售	VT- HJH-LPH-GJV减　JL-JYJL价 CLL-CL出　JL-V-HHHLH- LPH售	Jiaannjiaa Chushoou	Discount Sales
冷水	VT-JYV-PV冷　JPJY水	Leenng Shhuii	Cold Water
学生 票	VVJ-VP-PJH学 J-HHLH生 HLP-LLH-HH-JJV票	Xxuesheng Piaao	Student Tickets
酒吧	VVT-H LP-JCHH酒　LPH-PLHC吧	Jjiuuba	Cocktail Bar
海关	VVT-JH-CPVHV海　VJ-HHJY关	Hhaaiguan	Customs
浴室	VVT-JVJY-LPH浴　VVP-HCV-HLH室	Yuushi	Bath
油 漆 未 干	VVT-LPHLH油　　VVT-HLJY-JY- JVTJV漆　　HHLJY未　HHL干	Yyouqi Weei Gan	Paint Not Dry
游泳 池	VVT-VHJP-JHPJH游　VVT-VJPJY泳 VVT-PLC池	Yyouyoonng Chhivvt	Swimming Pool
请勿 乱扔	VZ-HHLH-LPHH请　JPJJ勿 JHL-LPH乱　HJT-ZJ扔	Qiinng Wuuj Luaanreng	Please No Littering
请勿 吐痰	VZ-HHLH-LPHH请　JPJJ勿 LPH-HLH吐　　VHJVT-VJJY-VJJY痰	Qiinng Wuuj Ttuutann	Please No Spitting
请勿 触 摸	VZ-HHLH-LPHH请　JPJJ勿 JP-JPHHL-LPHLHV触 HJT-HLL-LPHH- HJY摸	Qiinng Wuuj Chuumo	Please Don't Touch
请勿 入 内	VZ-HHLH-LPHH请　JPJJ勿 YJ入　LPJV内	Qiinng Wuuj Ruu Neei	Please Don't Enter
记念品	VZ-PHC记 JYVP-VCVV念 LPH-LPH-LPH品	Jiiniaan Piinn	Souvenirs
	W X Y Z		

▦™ TiENSTROKES ® USA
www.internetchinese.com * China Certificate of Standardization®1999 * www.tienstrokes.com

"BIRDS"	In TiENSTROKES CODE ALPHABETIC ORDER	Internet-Chinese	Internet-English
阳台	ZL-LPHH阳 CV-LPH台	Yanngttai	Terrace

SPECIAL NOTE:

Having gone through the above list of "CHINESE BIRDS", you are now ready to practice decoding some of the most commonly used Chinese characters 'flying' around airports, hotels, public buildings, restaurants, parks, zoos, gardens, newsstands or anywhere. Of course, you will have fun identifying these 'birds' and then confirming their true meanings with the above the TiENSTROKES, INTERNET-CHINESE-ENGLISH terms in the proper columns in the above table.

I. ACCELERATED LEARNING METHOD

This Internet-English speech order is an *accelerated learning* method that provides you with a learning team, a natural teacher and a student in 2 languages. That is, the TaxiTutor booklet will enable you to learn from a Beijing taxi driver and you as a customer. You can learn in a 'moving classroom', the taxicab on the go. To master the daily words and phrases more easily, meaningfully, literally and humorously, thereby remembering them better. By repetition with re-enforcement of the sounds and music in a world-class metropolis, your Chinese language learning can become exciting in Beijing, even in one-week tour. The useful idea is that, if you are going to Beijing, perchance, any taxi driver you hire becomes a natural Mandarin-speaking tutor. The course will also enable your Beijing taxi driver to speak in Internet-English to you. Beijing taxi drivers are being encouraged to learn English and to use this TaxiTutor is a new adventure in and by itself.

INTERNET-CHINESE LANGUAGE GUIDE

The Internet-Chinese language pronunciation is based on Mandarin, the common standard Beijing dialect, taught in all Chinese schools and spoken by over 85% of all Chinese people, nationwide and worldwide. Internet-Chinese script is the direct precise phonetization of Mandarin, using the Pinyin Latin alphabet. If you know the English Phonic Alphabet, you already know the Chinese Pinyin Alphabet, used in the Internet-Chinese format, separating the vowels from the consonants. They are basically the same in the global Vowel-Consonant Chart, as shown:

Internet-Chinese Vowel-Consonant Chart	
V = Vowels	**C = Consonants**
A a	Bb Cc Dd
E e	Ff Gg Hh
I i	Jj Kk Ll Mm Nn
O o	Pp Qq Rr Ss Tt
U u	Vv Ww Xx Yy Zz

English-Chinese Bilingual Vowel-Consonant Guide

English Phonic Alphabet						Chinese Pinyin Alphabet						Internet-Mandarin Pronunciation					
A	B	C	D			A	B	C	D			Ah	Bo	C=T's	Dir		
E	F	G	H			E	F	G	H			Eh	Fou	Gee	Hur		
I	J	K	L	M	N	I	J	K	L	M	N	I=Ee	Jee	Ke	Le	Mo	En
O	P	Q	R	S	T	O	P	Q	R	S	T	O=Wo	Po	Q=Chee	R=Z'r	Ss	Tur
U	V	W	X	Y	Z	U	V	W	X	Y	Z	U=Wu	Vi	Woa	X=She	Ya	Z=Dz

All the Chinese vowels and consonant letters are sounded similar to English ones, except for 4 letters, listed in the Chart: that is, c=t's, q=chee, r=z'r, x=she.

In order to transform the square Chinese characters precisely into an internationally readable Internet-Mandarin words, based the Pinyin alphabet, a general formula was sought, over a period of many years, to satisfy all challenging conditions:

The e-Chinese script must be equivalent to all aspects of square Chinese ideograms:

$$CC = PY + \bar{T}L + SL = IC$$

CC = Chinese character [square ideogram]
PY = Pinyin [letters]
SL = Stroke-letters
TL = Toneletters
IC = Internet-Chinese [linear e-script].

The Internet-Chinese language pronunciation is based on Mandarin, the common standard Beijing dialect, taught in all Chinese schools and spoken by over 85% of all Chinese people, nationwide and worldwide. Internet-Chinese script is the direct precise phonetization of Mandarin, using the Pinyin Latin alphabet. If you know the English Phonic Alphabet, you already know the Chinese Pinyin Alphabet, in the Internet-Chinese format, separating the vowels from the consonants. They are basically the same in the global Vowel-Consonant Chart, as shown:

INTERNET-CHINESE					
GLOBAL ALPHABET CHART					
Vowel /	Consonant Table				
A	B	C	D		
E	F	G	H		
I	J	K	L	M	N
O	P	Q	R	S	T
U	V	W	X	Y	Z
© 1961-2001 by H. C. Tien, M.D.					

The Internet-Chinese Alphabet and the English Alphabet are pronounced nearly same, except for 4 letters c q r x. And these 4 Chinese consonant letters, c q r x, *are pronounced c=t's, q=chee, r=zur, x=she*. They sound differently from the English letters. Ask your Mandarin-speaking taxi driver or a friend to sound them out for you. However, the 26 Pinyin letters do not carry the 4 tones in spelling each syllable, so a tone mark [- , /, ∨ or \ ] or a number [1, 2, 3 or 4] has to be added before the invention of the Internet-Chinese spelling, for example the syllable *ma* has four tones:

	PINYIN	+TONE-MARK	+TONE-NUMBER	+TONELETTER
1st Tone	ma	mā	ma-1	ma
2nd Tone	ma	má	ma-2	mma
3rd Tone	ma	mǎ	ma-3	mmaa
4th Tone	ma	mà	ma-4	maa

Whereas, the Internet-Chinese spelling, either Pinyin+ToneLetter or enhanced Pinyin+Toneletter+StrokeLetter, has been standardized as more precise equivalent to the square Chinese ideograms or Sinographs. The linearized Internet-Chinese script is more efficient in keyboard work and more meaningful than pure Pinyin with either tonemarks or tonenumbers. It contains more information as square Sinographs, unique in spelling words with variable tone letters, used in e-mail communications, hence its name, Internet-Chinese [IC]. IC is a breakthrough to the ambiguity problem of Chinese homophones. Linguistically, the toned spelling with an average of 3 stroke-letters reflects what's being spoken uniquely in Mandarin, and yet readable as a meaningful stand-alone ideogram character. When two ideograms are said together, they combine to become an Internet-Chinese word, like an English word. The spelling of every Internet-Mandarin word is fully pronounced as in Italian, and the silent French-like word endings are also eliminated in the process of polysyllabic word as in English.

V. INTERNET-CHINESE SCRIPT TRANSFORMATION

SCRIPT TRANSFORMATION IS THE CORE CONCEPT OF INTERNET-CHINESE SPELLING. Study the following evolving table, showing the actual transformation of the square Chinese characters into modern Internet-Mandarin [Ppuutonghuaa] script for e-Education and e-Communication. At the same time, e-transformation also accomplishes the miracle modern mastery of the ancient beautiful Ancient Chinese ideograms on the Cybernet by all who learn Internet-Chinese first. Here is a Table summarizing the modern Internet-Chinese language transformation in the 21st Century InfoCom Economy:

Ancient Ideogram circa 3000 - 6000 years		The Homo-phone Enigma	Pinyin Mono-Syllable with Tone-mark	Substitute with Tone-letters	Add initial Stroke-letters of an Ideogram as silent consonants, like in French, e.g. *les chats* [the cats]	Add a 2nd Ideogram (to produce the modern linearized polysyllabic e-words...⇦	Square Ancient Ideograms *to* Modern Internet-Chinese e-Words	Phoenician Indo-European *to* Current Internet-English e-Words
Complex - circa 1000 BC	Simplified - 1958							
媽	妈	ma-1	mā	ma	ma *cjh* = 妈	ma*cjh* 妈	妈妈 ⇔ mama	mother
麻	麻	ma-2	má	mma	mma *vhj* = 麻	fann*vjjv*= 烦	麻烦⇔ mmafann	trouble
馬	马	ma-3	mǎ	mmaa	mmaa *pzh* =马	lii*pj* =力	马力 ⇔ mmaalii	horsepower
罵	骂	ma-4	mà	maa	maa *lph* = 骂	le*pj* =了	骂了 ⇔ maale	scolded

© 1961-2001 H.C. Tien, M.D. , World Journal of Psychosynthesis

How to Read Internet-Chinese Words

Read the new transcribed complex Chinese <u>square</u> characters into linear Mandarin words. Pinyin syllables+Toneletters+ Stroke letters as <u>Linear</u> words of the modern Internet-Chinese script. Traditional square Characters usually have two parts, an articulated phonic and a silent graphic. With the three basic Internet-Chinese Rules, you are ready to sound out correctly any Internet-Mandarin word. And you are on your way toward speaking Mandarin and learning to spell Internet-Chinese e-mail directly on the Net, like so:

<u>Pronounce Internet-Chinese Words like English words,</u> yet quietly observe the *French rule*. That is, don't pronounce the consonants at the end. Now, you are now ready to read any Internet-Chinese words.
For examples:

You speak English? = Nniij shuovz Yingyyuu?
I speak Mandarin-Chinese. = Wwooj shuovz Ppuutonghuaa.
Oh, Good! = Ah, Hhaao!

田™ TiENSTROKES ® USA
www. internetchinese.com * China Certificate of Standardization®1999 * www.tienstrokes.com

New A-BCD Vowel-Consonant Song = Xinde Mmuuyin-Zziiyin A-BCD Ge

Column I		Column II		Column III		Column IV	
ENGLISH ALPHABET		**AMERICAN PRONUNCIATION**		**INTERNET-CHINESE ALPHABET**		**MANDARIN PRONUNCIATION**	
26 Phonic Letters		**Mandarin Phonics**		**Pinyin Letters**		汉语拼音字母表	
A	B C D	ah	bo t's dir	A	B C D	啊	玻 雌 得
E	F G H	uh	fou gir hur	E	F G H	鹅	佛 哥 喝
I	J K L	ea	jee ke ler mo en	I	J K L M N	衣	基 科 勒 摸 恩
O	P Q R S T	wo	po chee z'zr se tur	O	P Q R S T	喔	坡 欺 日 思 特
U	V W X Y Z	wu	vi wo she ya dz	U	V W X Y Z	呜	维 我 希 丫 子

© 1961-2001 by Dr. TiEN

Wwoomen Chaang		A	B	C	D	
We	**Sing**	**A**	**B**	**C**	**D**	
我们	唱	啊	玻	雌	得	
A	**B**	**C**	**D**			
啊	玻	雌	得			
6	|6	5	5	- |		
E	**F**	**G**	**H**			
鹅	佛	哥	喝			
5	|4	4	4	| 2	2	- |
I	**J**	**K**	**L**	**M**	**N**	
衣	基	科	勒	摸	恩	
5	|5	4	3	|3	2	- |
O	**P**	**Q**	**R**	**S**	**T**	
喔	坡	欺	日	思	特	
5	|5	4	3	|3	2	- |
U	**V**	**W**	**X**	**Y**	**Z**	
呜	维	我	希	丫	子	
4	4	| 3	2	2	1	- |
We sing	|	**A**	**B**	**C**	**D**	
Wwoomen chaang	|	**A**	**B**	**C**	**D**	
我们 唱	|	啊	玻	雌	得	

II. Shhibbiihuaa Ge 十笔画 歌 Tenstrokes Song
Tiann San Wenn Zhuutt,
[Tune after *Clementine*]

```
1 1  1  5.          |3 3 3 1            | 1 3 5 5        | 4.3  2 -|
十笔画 呀!          十笔画呀!           十笔画呀,         你有  什么?
ShhiBihua ya!   ShhiBihua ya!   ShhiBihua ya,        nnii  yyoou shennme
Oh, my   Tenstrokes, Oh, my Tenstrokes, Oh, my Tenstrokes,  what have you?
```

```
1 1  1  5.          |3 3 3 1        | 1 3 5 5       | 4.3  2 - |
V有点呀,             H 有 横呀,       L有竖呀,        J 有 撇呀,
V yyoou diaannya,   H yyoou henngya, L yyoou shuuya, J yyoou ppieeya,
V has a dot,        H has H-stroke,  L has L-stroke, J has J-stroke,
```

```
2  3 4 4      | 3  2  3 1     |1 3 2 5 .       | 7 2 1 - ||
我们 唱歌        我 们  跳舞      Y 变 捺呀,         哈哈哈!
Wwoomen chaangge, wwoomen tiaaowwuu, Y biaan naaya, Ha Ha Ha !
We    are singing,  we are dancing  Y has Y-stroke,    Ha Ha Ha !
```

```
1 1  1  5.     |3 3 3 1      | 1 3 5 5     | 4.3  2 -  |
十笔 画 呀!     十笔画 呀!     十笔画呀,      还有 什么?
ShhiBihua ya!   ShhiBihua ya!   ShhiBihua hhai ! yyoou shennme
Oh, my  Tenstrokes,  Oh, my  Tenstrokes, Oh, my Tenstrokes,  have you more?
```

```
1 1  1  5.          |3 3 3 1          | 1 3 5 5     | 4.3   2 - |
T有提  呀,           G有钩呀,          P有弯呀,       C 有  曲呀,
T yyoou ttiya,      G yyoou gouya,    P yyoou wanya, C yyoou quya,
T has T-stroke,     G  has G-stroke , P  has P-stroke, C has C-stroke,
```

```
2  3 4  4     | 3   2   3 1    |1 3 2 5 . | 7 2 1 - ||
我 们 唱 歌      我 们  跳 舞       Z 变 折呀, 哈哈 哈!
Wwoomen chaangge wwoomen tiaaowwuu  Z biaan zhheya  Ha Ha Ha
We   are singing,  we  are  dancing  Y has Y-stroke,  Ha Ha Ha !
```

```
1 1 1  5.           |3 3 3 1           |1 3 5 5        | 4.3  2 -|
十笔画呀!            十笔画 呀!           十笔 画呀!        我 爱你.
Oh, my  Tenstrokes, Oh, my Tenstrokes, Oh, my Tenstrokes, I love you
ShhiBihua ya!      ShhiBihua ya!      ShhiBihua ya!      wwooj aai nnii
```

INTRODUCTION TO INTERNET PHONIC-CHINESE SCRIPT
[1] TiENSTROKES Chinese Alphabet Exercise

Trace Chinese 10-Strokes	Pair with TiENSTROKES global Alphabet Letters	Give 10 English Letter Names	Say English Names	Write Global Alphabet strokes
`	` V	V dot	V-dot	`
一	一 H	H stroke	H-stroke	一
∣	∣ L	L stroke	L-stroke	∣
ノ	ノ J	J stroke	J-stroke	ノ
＼	＼ Y	Y stroke	Y-stroke	＼
⌐	⌐ T	T stroke	T-stroke	⌐
↳	↳ G	G stroke	G-stroke	↳
⌐|	⌐| P	P stroke	P-stroke	⌐|
⌊	⌊ C	C stroke	C-stroke	⌊
乙	乙 Z	Z stroke	Z-stroke	乙

English Exercise I: Say '**J stroke, H stroke, Y stroke**' ,
but write strokes ' ノ 一 ＼ '=> '**A**'□
Chinese Exercise I: Say '**H stroke, L-stroke, J stroke Y stroke**'
but write strokes ' 一 ∣ ノ ＼ '=> '木'
Now, you are writing both *phonic letters* and *graphic characters* with the same strokes of
TiENSTROKES® Global Alphabet.

Note: Master [1] the TiENSTROKES Chinese Alphabet; [2] the Global Alphabet Chart how to decode
Note: any English capital letters into TiENSTROKES; [3] how to
decode any Chinese ideograph with the same StrokeAlphabet. [4] to use Internet-Chinese ⇔ Internet-
English Dictionary (see Introduction to Internet-Chinese ⇔ Internet-English Script)

[2] GLOBAL ALPHABET CHART					
Vowel /	**Consonant Table**				
A	B	C ⌊	D		
E	F	G ↳	H 一		
I	J ノ	K	L ∣	M	N
O	P ⌐|	Q	R	S	T ⌐
U	V `	W	X	Y ＼	Z 乙

You Can Now Practice On Internet-Chinese Mandarin spelling and reading with knowledge and
experience gained in playing the 3 SpellChecker Games and the "BIRD WATCHING GAME".

To check the alphabetic spellings of Phonic-Chinese script or
Internet-Chinese words used in the TiENSTROKES Games I, II & III
For your fun and convenience visit www.internetchinese.com

INTERNET-CHINESE PINXXIEE ORTHOGRAPHY

This orthography is <u>Internet-Chinese Mandarin spelling</u>, described below. It is based on spelling Chinese characters with all alphabetic LETTERS in Pinyin+Tone+Stroke, in order to make each ideograph uniquely spelled. Having solved the 4-tone problem with letters, rather than tone marks or tone numbers, the author was able to formally propose in the *World Journal of Psychosynthesis* in 1969, a Pinxxiee Theory of transforming square Chinese Characters (Sinographs) from a square format to a linear alphabetic format, like so,

拼写 = 拼音 + 拼调 + 拼形 = 方 块 汉字

Pinxxiee = Pinyin + Pindiaao + Pinxinng = Fangkuaai Haanzii

Pinxxiee = Spellphonic + Spelltone + Spellstroke = Square Sinography

In 1999, this Pinxxiee Orthography was certified by China Standardization Association as the standardized Internet-Chinese Script, a linear alternate form of Traditional Chinese Characters (Square Sinography). The following table is published here, showing the actual transformation of the square Chinese characters into modern Internet-Mandarin script of General Dialect [Ppuutonghuaa] for e-Education and e-Communication. At the same time, e-transformation also accomplishes the miracle modern mastery of the ancient beautiful Ancient Chinese ideograms on the Cybernet by all who learn Internet-Chinese first. Here is a Table summarizing the modern Internet-Chinese language transformation with e-InfoCom Economy in the 21st Century:

Ancient Ideogram circa 3000 - 6000 years		The Homo-phone Enigma	Pinyin Mono-Syllable with Tone-mark	Pinxxiee Substitute with Tone-letters	Spell an Ideogram by Pinxxiee StrokeLetters stroke-by-stroke as silent radicals	Add a toned syllable to a silent radical of a given Ideogram to produce a modern linearized word ⇔ like in French, e.g. *chat* [cat]	Square Ancient Ideogram *to* Modern Internet-Chinese e-Word	Phoenician Indo-European *to* Current Internet-English e-Words
Complex - circa 1000 BC	Simplified - 1958							
媽	妈	ma-1	mā	ma	cjh *cjh* = 妈	ma*cjh* ⇔ 妈	macjh	mother
麻	麻	ma-2	má	mma	*vhj* hljvhljy= 麻	mmavhj⇔ 麻	mmavhj	hemp
馬	马	ma-3	mǎ	mmaa	*pzh* =马	mmaapzh⇔马	mmaa	horse
罵	骂	ma-4	mà	maa	*lph* lph pzh= 骂	maalph⇔骂	maalph	scold

The applications of Internet-Chinese script are numerous. For instance, *Language Companion* using this script allows the Mandarin-speaking taxi driver and English-speaking traveler to exchange information quickly and to learn by Internet-Chinese script and motion of hands or pointing at the square characters in the *Language Companion* ™ The practical usefulness of accelerated learning in real personal tutoring in a taxicab. Users of the TaxiTutor™ should feel at ease about accepting alternative sentence translations from other native speakers of each other's language.

THE INTERNET-CHINESE SCRIPT serves as an essential and much needed linguistic bridge between *Phonic-English* and *Graphic-Chinese* scripts, in their respective minds and cultures, on or off the Net. Internet-English and Internet-Chinese will rapidly become equally important tourist languages in the coming seven years, when the Summer Olympic Games run around to Beijing, China by 2008. It is timely for Americans to learn Internet-Chinese, and Chinese, English, people are having fun building friendship as we are flying back and forth between U.S. and China, now.

ENGLISH AND CHINESE ALPHABETS COMPARED

The two alphabets, English and Chinese are identical twins. If you know one, you recognize the other one, only with different names. If you know the English Alphabet, then you know the modern Internet-Chinese Alphabet, automatically. Learn the pronunciation of the Chinese phonics and graphics of this twin Alphabet, by studying the above table. The American phonics are in column II. Note only 4 Chinese Pinyin letters, CRQX, sound somewhat differently to the American ear. [Mnemonic: 'CRUX' recalls C R Q X!]. Remember C sounds like 't's', R like 'zz'r' , Q like 'chee', and X like 'she'. To gain confidence, listen to the audiocassette that accompanies your TaxiTutor™ Internet-Chinese *Language Companion*.

There are also 3 more 'retroflexes' of double-consonants: zh; ch; and sh. They are pronounced like so: zh as 'j' like in 'jut'; ch as in 'chur'; sh as in 'ssh', respectively. If you know the 26 letters of the Chinese Alphabet sound like English, then you have already learned the basic Pinyin spelling of Mandarin, spoken by 85-90% of the Chinese population; and taught 100% in Chinese elementary and middle schools; and used in all high schools and colleges throughout the People's Republic of China. To speak and spell more accurately, you will be happy to know *your* Chinese Language Companion teaches you how to spell the 4 tones, that will enable you to read and write the common dialect like a Beijing Mandarin native.

THE NEW TONE-LETTER MTHOD OF SPELLING MANDARIN SYLLABLES

In 1969, the author introduced *tone-letters*, akin to the ancient Greeks adding vowel-letters [e.g. a, i] to bare consonants [e.g. Dvd] to complete syllabic spelling [e.g. David], as in modern English. Before the invention of tone-letters in Internet-Chinese spelling, the 26 PHONIC letters do not spell the 4 tones, inherent in each Mandarin syllable. So, a Tone mark [$-$, $/$, $\vee$ or $\setminus$] or a number [1, 2, 3 or 4] had to be added. The extra Tone-mark or Arabic number is not alphabetic. Differently toned Mandarin words need to be spelled out differently, all with alphabetic letters to be readable: e.g. the syllable ' *ma*' has four toned words, which has 4 different meanings: SEE:

How to Use Tone-Letters to Spell Mandarin Syllables Naturally

TONES	PINYIN	+TONE-MARK	+TONE-NUMBER	+TONE-LETTER	MEANINGS
1st Tone	ma	mā	ma-1	ma	mother
2nd Tone	ma	má	ma-2	mma	hemp
3rd Tone	ma	mǎ	ma-3	mmaa	horse
4th Tone	ma	mà	ma-4	maa	curse

SPECIAL APPENDIX for
ENGLISH-SPEAKING MANDARIN TEACHERS

For TEACHERS AND PARENTS WHO KNOW HOW TO SPEAK MANDARIN, USING THIS BOOKLET AS AN TUTORIAL FOR PHONIC-CHINESE OR INTERNET-CHINESE classes to teach barrier-free e-mailing or word processing in preparing lessons, papers or articles with readable Mandarin-Chinese e-scripts, before converting to the traditional square Chinese ideographic characters, when needed:

1. THEORY:

(A) Phonic-Chinese = Pinyin + Toneletter = Fangkuaai Haanzii (Practice: 90% accuracy in conversion with software)

or

(B) Internet-Chinese = Pinyin + Toneletter + Strokeletters = Fangkuaai Haanzii (Practice: 95% accuracy in conversion with software)

or

(C) Internet-Chinese Pinxxiee = Pinyin + Toneletter+ Radicals = Fangkuaai Haanzii (Practice: 99+% accuracy in conversion with software)

2. PRACTICE:

The 10 Steps to Learn
the Basic Internet-Chinese Tenstrokes® Alphabet and Pinxxiee Radicals

The Tenstrokes letters, VHLJY TGPCZ, are used to spell radical suffixes, H *for* 一; L *for* 丨, etc.... Please note that the other consonants can thus be used, for example, by combining two stroke radicals H= 一. L= 丨 into a new radical –⊡= - t . This natural condensation of strokes into new radicals will become clear as you learn how the other radicals are so formed. Meanwhile, let's go to the first step:

STEP 1: LEARN TIENSTROKES. THAT IS, READ:

V-stroke =V 丶
H-stroke =H 一
L-stroke =L 丨
J-stroke =J 丿
Y-stroke = Y 丶
T-stroke = T ⌒
G-stroke = G 亅
P-stroke = P ⅂
C-stroke = C ∟
Z-stroke = Z 乙

⊞™ TiENSTROKES ® USA
www. internetchinese.com * China Certificate of Standardization®1999 * www.tienstrokes.com

So, you associate the 10 English letters with the 10 Chinese strokes in your memory as the Tenstrokes Alphabet*. *Note:* <u>V</u> 、 <u>H</u> 一 <u>L</u> 丨 <u>J</u> 丿 <u>Y</u> 丶 <u>T</u> ⼂ <u>G</u> ⼃ <u>P</u> 乛 <u>C</u> ⼌ <u>Z</u> 乙 are the modern letter names of the ten ancient strokes, the silent graphic stroke letters of the Global Alphabet.

TiENSTROKES Mnemonic is The Consonant letters within a girl's name Vi Holijoy, and a boy's name, Togo Picaz = ⇔ V H L J Y, T G P C Z ⇔ <u>V</u>、,<u>H</u>一,<u>L</u>丨,<u>J</u>丿,<u>Y</u>丶,<u>T</u>⼂,<u>G</u>⼃,<u>P</u>乛,<u>C</u>⼌,<u>Z</u>乙).

STEP 2: READ & WRITE TIENSTROKES.

#	STROKES	LETTER-STROKE NAME IN ENGLISH/ INTERNET-CHINESE	STROKE DESCRIPTION	3 EXAMPLES OF STROKES= CHARACTER = INTERNET-CHINESE	MEANINGS STROKES= CHARACTER= INTERNET-ENGLISH
0	、	V-stroke= V-diaann	V-dot 、 as in ⇔	VHJY=文 =wenn VVHL=斗 = doou VPY=之 = zhi	VHJY= 文 = script VVHL 斗 =fight VPY 之 = 's or of
1	一	H-stroke = H-henng	Horizontal 一 line as in ⇔	H一 = yih HH 二 = eer HHH 三= san	H一 = one HH 二 = two HHH 三 = three
2	丨	L-stroke = L-shuu	Longitudinal 丨 line as in ⇔	LLPHH = 旧 =jiuul LPH = 口 = kkoou LJHLPL = 师 =shilj	LLPHH 旧 = old LPH 口 = mouth LJHLPL 师 = tutor
3	丿	J-stroke = J-ppiee	J-stroke 丿 to the left as in ⇔	JYH = A = A JC =儿 =err JJGVY = 瓜 = gua	JYH = A = A JC =儿 = child JJGVY= 瓜 = melon
4	丶	Y-stroke =Y-naa	Y-stroke 丶 to the right as in ⇔	JY=人 = renn YJ =入 = ruu HJY= 大 = daa	JY=人 = person YJ =入 = into HJY= 大 = big
5	⼂	T-stroke =T-tti	Tick-up ⼂ to the right as in ⇔	VT=次 = cii VVT= 江 = jiang VVTCJH = 汝 = ruuv	VT=次 = next VVT= 江 = river VVTCJH =汝= thy
6	⼃	G-stroke = G-gou	Gash down ⼃ sharp right up as in ⇔	GVJV =以 = yyii HGJV=戈 = ge JPG JJPY饭= faan	GVJV =以 = use HGJV=戈 = spear JPG JJPY饭= meal
7	乛	P-stroke = P-wan	Pushing right 乛 then down as in ⇔	PLH =卫 = weeip JPC =勹= gou PHC =己 =jjiip	PLH =卫 = defend JPC =勹= connect PHC =己 = self
8	⼌	C-stroke =C-qu	Curve down ⼌ then right as in ⇔	CJH =女 = nneuu CCJ =乡 = xiangc CCC = 巛 = chuanc	CJH =女 = female CCJ =乡 =rural CCC= 巛 = stream
9	乙	Z-stroke = Z-zhhe	Zigzag 乙 in 2 directions as in ⇔	ZJV =飞 = feiz VZY=辶 = zzoouzhi PHZ =弓 = gongp	ZJV =飞 =flying VZY=辶 = going PHZ =弓 = bow

*Historical Notes: From 1961-96, the author conducted many experiments with initial letters of 10 English names,V-stroke H-stroke L-stroke J-stroke Y-stroke T-stroke G-stroke P-stroke C-stroke Z-strokefor 10 Chinese stroke names, V-diaann=点 H-henng=横 L-shuu=竖 J-ppiee =撇 Y-naa=捺 T-tti=提 G-gou=钩 P-wan =弯 C-qu=曲 Z-zhhe= 折 and resulted in the standardization of all ancient Chinese strokes into 10 basic forms,、 一 丨 丿 丶 ⼂ ⼃ 乛 ⼌ 乙 which not only most resembled in whole or in part of the 10 respective English letters,V H L J Y T G P C Z but can also *spell* any and all 60,000+ Chinese characters, the 26 English letters and the other Indo-European alphabets with the same 10 basic strokes. Therefore, Tenstrokes qualify as a global alphabet, the Transcode for spelling both phonic as well as for graphic scripts of the world. Tenstrokes thus emerged scientifically as a standardized Global Alphabet and was granted patents both in China and in the United States.TSW/HCT

STEP 3: KNOW TENSTROKES AS CONSONANTS.

Remember that only consonants are used to simulate strokes and radicals. Study the Vowel-Consonant relationship in the Table below:

Vowel-Consonant Alphabet Table

VOWELS	CONSONANTS				
A	B	_C_	D		
E	F	_G_	_H_		
I	_J_	K	_L_	M	N
O	_P_	Q	R	S	_T_
U	_V_	W	X	_Y_	_Z_

The Tenstrokes consonant letters, VHLJY TGPCZ, are used to spell radical suffixes, -h *for* ⼀, -l *for* 丨, etc....

Please note that the other remaining consonants can also thus be used, for example, by combining two stroke radicals -h-l, ⼀ 丨, into a new radical 十=-t. This natural condensation of strokes into new radicals will become clear, as you learn how radicals are so formed. Meanwhile, let's go to the next step.

STEP 4: LEARN TO SPELL TONES WITH LETTERS.

That is, remove all 4 tone marks ¯ / V \ on the selected vowel. Now, spell tones with letters, based on each syllable's consonant and/or vowel letters. That is, double the selected consonant to increase tone or double the selected vowel letter to decrease tone, indicating the 4 tones in any given syllable. An example will make this obvious as follows:

1st tone	*tian*	天
2nd tone	*tiann*	田
3rd tone	*tiaann*	舔
4th tone	*tiaan*	掭

The author's Double-letter spelling technique is an organic and logical solution of indicating the 4 tones ¯ / V \ of Putonghua (Mandarin), consistently and universally, for all characters. It is beyond the mechanical addition of 4 numbers, 1-2-3-4 or the arbitrary insertion of letters, a-ar-aa-ah for ā á ǎ à , to indicate the same 4 tones, ¯ / V \, as in *tian* syllable.

The Letter-doubling technique is based on neurolinguistics, that is to say, <u>consonants</u> are used to <u>increase</u> the frequency of a tone; and <u>vowels</u> are used to <u>decrease</u> the frequency of a tone, as the syllable is being produced by the speaker's voice.

™ TiENSTROKES ® USA
www. internetchinese.com * China Certificate of Standardization®1999 * www.tienstrokes.com

STEP 5: OBSERVE THE _N-RULE._ _VERY USEFUL RULE._

If a syllable contains the letter _n_, _e.g._ as in the syllable _tian,_ remove all tone marks, then observe:

1st tone remains the same: _tia<u>n</u>;_
2nd-tone shows a double-_nn: tia<u>nn</u>;_
3rd tone, double-_nn_ and double-_vowel: tia<u>ann</u>;_
4th tone, only double-_vowel: tia<u>an</u>._

This observation applies to many syllables in Mandarin, i.e., ban, bang, ben, beng, bian, bin, bing, can, cang, cen, ceng, chan, chang, chen, cheng, chong, chuan, chuang, chun, cong, cuan, cun, chen, and many other Putonghua syllables. As a matter of fact, about 40% of all Mandarin syllables contain the letter _n_ in its Pinyin spelling. Once learned, the n-rule can be widely used and effectively applied.

STEP 6: LEARN TO SPELL IN COMPUTER-CHINESE.

Computer-Chinese Script has 3 ever-improving Pinxxiee Orthography. That is, to advance beyond pure Pinyin Scheme, Dr. Tien has helped Chinese Language Commission to evolve the phonetic methods from Pinyin, decreed by Chinese Government in 1958 to a standard Internet-Chinese Script, announced in 1999 by China Standardization Association. The announcement states that Dr. Tien's Internet-Chinese electronic script (e-Chinese) R&D over the last 30 years emerged clearly in 3 stages, averaging 10 years per stage, fulfills governmental language requirements, as follows:

(A) The Phonic-Chinese stage, 1958 to 1968
(B) The Phonigraphic Pinxxiee stage, 1968 to 1978
(C) The Internet-Chinese Pinxxiee stage, 1988 to 1998, to achieve

(A)汉语 拼音拼调普通话=>
(B)因特网拼音拼调拼形中文=>
(C)汉语汉字拼写[音素＋形素]正字法).

Any Mandarin-speaking person can quickly and methodically learn to spell in Phonic-Mandarin, then improving to the Internet-Chinese script and arriving at the Phonic-Chinese Internet-Chinese Pinxxiee Orthography in a short time, depending on usage on the Internet. Pinxxiee Orthography as awarded the Certificate of Standardization on November 5, 1999, by China Standardization Association, as NEW practical Chinese _Internet-Chinese_ electronic-communication script, an alternative script to the _traditional_ Chinese ideographic script and to the _de facto_ Internet-English script as _lingua franca_ on the WorldWideWeb or WaanWweiWaanng [WWW].

In fact, if you know Mandarin Chinese, if you know Pinyin, and if you know TiENSTROKES Global Alphabet, then you already know how to spell basic Internet-Chinese script. The resultant Internet – Chinese script is a phonic script and, superficially resembles phonic French script or phonic English script. At last, they are all now in the same Global Alphabet™ linguistic domain. Foreigners, like English-speaking westerners, can now truly master both Phonic-Chinese and Graphic-Chinese, in both spoken as well as written Chinese scripts. That is to say, the Internet Phonic-Chinese as well as the square

Graphic-Chinese scripts can be taught with the same Tenstrokes ® Global Alphabet ™. At long last, Americans can now learn and teach Phonic-Mandarin with similar accelerated learning methods as they would learn and teach phonic French. [Just an aside: Who is the one who said, "The best way to Beijing is through Paris?"]

Pinxxiee means to spell Pinyin syllable with a tone letter to separate tian = 天, for instance, from: tiann = 田,but to further separate characters with the same tones, for example,

甜 & 恬 => tiann & tiann.

we must add 1-6 stroke-letters to the toned syllable, in order to separate homophonic-homotonic characters, e.g.

甜 =>tiann<u>jhl</u> & 恬 => tiann<u>vlv,</u>

like so, -<u>jtd</u>=-<u>jhl</u> & -<u>vlv</u>= 忄 as suffixes to spell differently from the basic radical-less homotonic homophone, tiann = 田.

When you learn 50+ such radicals -jtd = 舌 & -vlv = 忄，whose initial stroke letters like -jhl or -vlv, (consult Radical Suffix Table) you will be able to touch-type uniquely 90+% of ordinary text.

(The Radical Suffix Table is under Tenstrokes Program of Learning Common Radicals)

STEP 7: LEARN TO SPELL TWO-SYLLABLE WORDS.

In Pinxxiee, to spell 2-syllable compound words, remove radical suffix letters and spell as one word.

Example:
妹＋妹 => meeixx + meeixx => meeimeei => 妹妹

STEP 8: LEARN TO SPELL THREE-SYLLABLE WORDS.

In Pinxxiee, to spell 3-syllable compound words, remove radical suffix letters, and spell as one word:

Example: 联＋合＋国 => liann<u>ntht</u> + h<u>hejy</u> + gguo<u>q</u> => <u>**LiannHheGguo**</u> => 联合国 <=**United Nations**. And further remove both the radical suffix letters AND tone letters, and spell as one word, the spelling becomes TonlessPinyin™: liann<u>ntht</u> + h<u>hejy</u> + gguo<u>q</u> => <u>**LiannHeGuo**</u> => 联合国 <=**United Nations**; And, further abbreviation of the spelling becomes: <u>**LiannHeGuo**</u> => <u>**LHG**</u> => 联合国 <=**UN**.

STEP 9: PRACTICE ON PX2001 TUTOR. PRACTICE MAKES PERFECT.

To master Pinyin+tones and 50+ Pinxxiee radicals, use PX2001 Tutor, designed for self-teaching and learning. *You are now ready to take Step Ten!*

STEP 10: LEARN THE COMPUTER-CHINESE LANGUAGE

That is, to truly touch-type Haanzii => 汉字,*alphabetically, as in English or better still, as in French, with or without silent suffixes.* What does this mean? You can e-mail directly In Internet-Chinese script! to e-mail and to word-process in Internet-Chinese Pinxxiee script,
Use Internet-script to e-mail or to communicate with Mandarin-Chinese speakers and enter
Computer-Chinese World =>Diaan-nnaao Zhongwenn Shiijiee=> 电脑中文世界!

田™ TiENSTROKES ® USA
www. internetchinese.com * China Certificate of Standardization®1999 * www.tienstrokes.com

Entrance Prerequisites: Knowledge of Pinyin,* Chinese characters, and typing on regular keyboard. No special hardware or software needed to write Internet-Chinese script, if you are already emailing in English or similar scripts.

OBJECTIVE:

(Learning Time: Depending on previous training and experience.) Learn to *truly* touch-type Internet-Chinese, just like English or French. And Internet-Chinese is readable like English is readable. When needed the Internet-Chinese e-mail or e-communications can be converted accurately to Chinese ideographic characters or Haanzii => 汉字, *automatically, at the touch of button.*

For more information or introductory tutorial software: Visit Peking University Elementary School or Chinese Computer Communications, Inc. website: www.bdfx.net.cn or www.internetchinese.com

*[新华字典], Xinhhua Ziidiaann, Shangwu Yinshuguan, 商务印书馆, 1988，北京，中国

This Radical List is based on the Tenstrokes® Pinxxiee formula: (See Tenstrokes Pinxxiee Primer)

Chinese Character	= English letters	+ Tone letter + Graphic letters
= Computer Chinese		
门	= Men + n	+ lvp = Mennlvp (Gate-lvj)

The practical value of the Tenstrokes Pinxxiee ("pin-shay" = phonetics + graphics) Language Technology is both for education and for computer applications of the multilingual information industry.

1) **In 10 minutes** you can learn the English-Chinese Tenstrokes Global Alphabet pairs:

   V、   H一   L丨   J丿   Y丶   T一   G乚   P乛   C乚   Z乙

The best way to remember this is to play the *Chinese Tenstrokes® Game* from CCC.

2) **In 10 hours** you can learn to read the Tenstrokes in any Chinese character and decode to English letters, e.g., 木 => HLJY => Tree. The *Chinese Tenstrokes® Game* is a fun way to master this key tool with a teacher, by yourself, and/or with friends.

3) **In 10 days** you can learn the Tenstrokes PX Primer to truly touch-type any Chinese character (see "Table").

BASIC TiENSTROKES PINYIN+ PINXXIEE RADICAL TABLE

TENSTROKES RADICAL	HAANZII 笔画/汉字	PINXXIEE RADICAL	PINYIN+TONE NAME	PINXXIEE SCRIPT PROPER	ENGLISH RADICAL NAME
V	、 点	-v	V-bbiihuaa	V=Diaann	V-stroke
H	一 横	-h	H-bbiihuaa	H=Henngh	H-stroke
L	丨 竖	-l	L-bbiihuaa	L=Shuuvhvvh	L-stroke
J	丿 撇	-j	J-bbiihuaa	J=Ppieetx	J-stroke
Y	丶 捺	y-	Y-bbiihuaa	Y=Naatx	Y-stroke
T	一 提	t-	T-bbiihuaa	T=Ttitx	T-stroke
G	乚 钩	-g	G-bbiihuaa	G=Gouyhth	G-stroke
P	乛 弯	p-	P-bbiihuaa	P=Wan	P-stroke
C	乚 曲	-c	C-bbiihuaa	C=Qu	C-stroke
Z	乙 折	-z	Z-bbiihuaa	Z=Zhhetx	Z-stroke
CCH	纟	-cch	Jjiaaosi-pann	Jiaosipang	Twisted-silk-radical
CJH	女	-xx	Nneuu-ziipannng	Neuzipang	Female-radical
HCHL	车	-xtx	Che-ziipannng	Chezipang	Car-radical
HHLH	王	-hth	Wanng	Wanngh	King
HJ-LP-JY	页	-tmy	Yee	Yeetmy	Page

TENSTROKES RADICAL	HAANZII 笔画/汉字	PINXXIEE RADICAL	PINYIN+TONE NAME	PINXXIEE SCRIPT PROPER	ENGLISH RADICAL NAME
HJT	扌	-tx	Ttishhoou-panng	Tishoupang	Lifthand
HJV	寸	-tj	Cuun	Cuuntj	Inch
HJY	大	-hy	Daa	Daahy	Big
HLJY	木	-tv	Muu	Muuhljy	Tree
HLL	艹	-tt	Ccaao-ziittou	Caozitou	Grass-header
HLPL-VVVV	雨	-tmhh	Yyuu	Yyuutmhh	Rain
JH-HHG	钅	-yhth	Jin-ziipanng	Jinzipang	Gold
JHHJ	手	-jtj	Shhoou	Shhooujtj	Hand
JHHL	牛	-jtt	Nniu	Nniujtt	Oxen
J-HLJY	禾	-jtv	Hhe	Hhejtv	Cereal
JHL-LPH	舌	-jtd	Shhe	Shhejtd	Tongue
JHV-JHV	竹	-kk	Zhhu	Zhhukk	Bamboo
JJL	彳	-yy	Shuangrenn	Shuangrenn	Two-person
JL	亻	-y	Danrenn	Danrenn	One-person
JPG	饣	-hv	Shhi	Shhihv	Feed
JPHH	月	-mhh	Yuee/Roou	Yuee/Roou	Moon/Meat
JPJ	犭	-xjj	Quaann	Quaannxjj	Canine
JPJY	水	-sk	Shhuii	Shhuiisk	Water
JP-LPHLH-H	鱼	-jjdth	Yyu	Yyujjdth	Fish
JPVZH	鸟	-jpvzh	Nniaao	Nniaaojpvzh	Bird
LCL	山	-w	Shan	Shanw	Hill
LJ	刂	-lj	Liidao	Liidao	Vertical-knife
LPH	口	-d	Kkoou	Kkooud	Mouth
LPHH	日	-dh	Rii	Riidh	Sun
LP-HL-H	田	-dt	Tiann	Tianndt	Fields
LPH-LH-JY	足	-dty	Zzu	Zzudty	Foot
LPH-LHV	虫	-dlhv	Chonng	Chonngdlhv	Crawler
LP-JY	贝	-my	Beei	Beeimy	Cowrie
LPL	巾	-ml	Jin-ziibuu	Jinzibu	Kerchief
LVP	门	-lvp	Menn	Mennlvp	Door
PJ	力	-xj	Lii	Liixj	Power
PL	卩	-p	Dan-eerr	Daneerr	One-ear
PZH	马	-pzh	Mmaa	Mmaapzh	Horse
VCVV	心	-vcvv	Xin	Xinvcvv	Heart
VHJ	广	-vhj	Guaanng	Guaanngvhj	Broad
VHJVV	疒	-vhjvv	Biing	Biingvhjvv	Sick
VHJY	文	-vhx	Wenn	Wennvhz	Script
VLV	忄	-vlv	Shuuxin	Shuuxin	Vertical-heart
VPLVV	衤	-vplvv	Yi	Yivplvv	Coat
VV-HLJY	米	-xt	Mmii	Mmiixt	Rice
VVJY	火	-vk	Hhuoo	Hhuoovk	Fire
VVP	宀	-vm	Bbaaogaai	Baogaier	Treasure's-cover
VVT	氵	-s	Sandianshui	Sandianshui	3-drops-of-water
VVVV	灬	-vvvv	Siidiaann	Siidiaann	4-dots
VZ	讠	-vz	Yann	Yannvz	Talk
VZY	辶	-vzy	Zzoouzhi	Zzoouzhi	Going
ZL	阝	-b	Erduopang	Erduopang	Ear-radical

⊞™ TiENSTROKES ® USA
www. internetchinese.com * China Certificate of Standardization®1999 * www.tienstrokes.com

SUMMARY: The <u>Ten Steps to Master the Basics of Tenstrokes Pinxxiee Computer-Chinese Language</u>

Prerequisites: Knowledge of Pinyin, Chinese characters, and typing on regular keyboard.
Objective: Learn to <u>*truly*</u> touch-type Haanzii => 汉字 <u>*alphabetically*</u>. (Learning Time: 10-15 hr.)

INTRODUCTION

1. Theory:	Pinxxiee	=	Pinyin	+ Tone	+ Radical	<=> Haanzii
2. Practice:	Haanzii	=	Pinyin Syllables	+ Tone Letters	+ Radical Suffix	<=> 汉字
3. Formula:	PX	=	PY	+ T	+ R	<=> HZ
Example:	*yiidh*	=	*yi*	+ *I*	+ *dh*	= 易

<u>Step One.</u> Learn that all 60,000+ Chinese characters can be written with only Tenstrokes:

0	1	2	3	4	5	6	7	8	9
丶	一	丨	丿	乀	乁	乚	𠃌	乚	乙

<u>Step Two.</u> Pair the 10 strokes with 10 letters to create the Tenstrokes Alphabet*.

That is:	V 丶	H 一	L 丨	J 丿	Y 乀	T 乁	G 乚	P 𠃌	C 乚	Z 乙
Read:	V-stroke	H-stroke	L-stroke	J-stroke	Y-stroke	T-stroke	G-stroke	P-stroke	C-stroke	Z-stroke

<u>Step Three.</u> Tenstrokes letters are consonants and only consonants are used to simulate strokes and radicals. Master the Vowel-Consonant relationship in the Pinyin/Pinxxiee Alphabet Table below:

	A	B	*C*	D			
	E	F	*G*	*H*			
Vowels	I	*J*	K	*L*	M	N	**Consonants**
	O	*P*	Q	R	S	*T*	
	U	*V*	W	X	*Y*	*Z*	

<u>Step Four.</u> Double consonant and/or vowel letters to indicate the 4 tones of Putonghua (Mandarin).
That is, remove all tone marks and spell tones with letters as follows, for example:
1st Tone: tian 天; 2nd tone: tiann 田; 3rd tone: tiaann 舔; 4th: tiaan 掭.

<u>Step Five.</u> Observe the *n-rule*: if a syllable, e.g. <u>*tian*</u>, contains the letter *n* in its 1st tone, then the 2nd-tone always shows a double-*nn*; third tone, double-*nn* and double-*vowel*; and 4th tone, only double-*vowel*.

<u>Step Six:</u> Add radical letters, to separate other homophones with same syllable & tone, for instance, 甜 & 恬, tiann<u>jtd</u> = 甜 & tiann<u>vlv</u> = 恬; using -jtd=舌 & -vlv=忄 suffixes to separate homophones. And Learn 50+ such radicals like -jtd = 舌 and -vlv = 忄 and that will cover 90+% of ordinary text. (The Radical Suffix Table is on the "Tenstrokes Program of Learning Common Radicals".)

<u>Step Seven:</u> Remove radical suffix letters, to spell 2-syllable compound words:
Example: meeixx + meeixx => meeimeei => 妹妹

<u>Step Eight:</u> Remove both radical suffix and tone letters, to spell 3-syllable compound words:
Example: 联+ 合 +国 => liannthht+hhejv+gguoq => <u>Liannhhegguo</u> ⇔ 联合国, which can be further abbreviated to LianHeGuo ⇔ LHG ⇔ UN ⇔ 联合国

<u>Step Nine.</u> Use CCC PX2001 Tutor and learn Pinyin+ and 50+ Pinxxiee radicals to touch-type 汉字.
<u>Step Ten.</u> Use CCC Pinyin+Pinxxiee Input System for Windows and enter Computer-Chinese World, 电脑中文世界!

**Note:

V	H	L	J	Y	T	G	P	C	Z	are the modern letter names of the ten ancient strokes, which
❣	一	丨	丿	乀	乁	乚	𠃌	乚	乙	are the silent graphic stroke letters of Pinxxiee alphabet

Mnemonic Password: Vi HoLiJoY; ToGo PiCaZ.
Vi Holijoy is a girl's name; and Togo Picaz is a boy's name. Or, you may create your own mnemonic.

十笔画综合[拼音+拼写]=
[汉语拼音方案+汉字拼写方案(草案)] =>
成为 电脑因特网-中文.

提先准备: 能用[新华字典]** 加三会：会拼音；会键盘；会指法. (学习时间: 10-15小时.)
目的：学习电脑中文，即可以准确地按指法盲打和快打汉字象打英文或法文一样方便。

简介

1. 理论: 拼写 = 拼音 + 声调 + 部首 =汉字
2. 实践: 拼写单字 = 拼音音节 + 声调字母 + 部首字母 =电脑中文
3. 公式: **PX** = **PY** + **SD** + **BS** = **HZ**

*例： **yiidh** = **yi** + **i** + **dh** =易*

十步骤(*Shhi Buulhlh Zhooupzh*) 掌握 拼写电脑中文

<u>第一步</u>。理解历史上所有的 60,000+ 汉字的笔画都能归类为十笔：

0 1 2 3 4 5 6 7 8 9

点 横 竖 撇 捺 提 钩 弯 曲 折

十笔画可以在电脑上拼写任何汉字, 包括汉语拼音字母 ABC...XYZ.
<u>第二步</u>。把十笔画同十个拼音字母配对成十笔画世界字母*.
即：V 、；H 一；L 丨；J 丿；Y 乀；T 乚；G 乚；P 𠃌；C ㄥ；Z 乙.
读: V-bihua; H-bihua; L-bihua; J-bihua; Y-bihua; T-bihua; G-bihua; P-bihua; C-bihua; Z-bihua.
<u>第三步</u>。十笔画完全是子音字母，只有子音字母才能仿写中文笔画和部首。掌握母音、子音的功能，▬
浐叵岛芟悦韩睦　谄匆簟(2)葱醋帜副砝锶缦▬:

母音= **Mmuuyin= Vowel**	子音= **Zziiyin = Consonant**					
A	B	*C*	D			
E	F	*G*	*H*			
I	*J*	K	*L*	M	N	
O	*P*	Q	R	S	*T*	
U	*V*	W	X	*Y*	*Z*	

<u>第四步</u>。复写子音字母或母音字母来表示汉语拼音(普通话)的声调，
采用拼音+加复写字母来区别4个声调，同时删掉4个声调符号 - / ∨ \，如下：
第1声:不加. 第2声:加子音(升其调). 第3声: 加母子音(降升其调). 第4声:加母音(降其调).
一声: tian 天 ；二声: tiann 田 ；三声: tiaann 舔 ；四声: tiaan 掭。
<u>第五步</u>. 复写子音字母声调规则：如果一个音节:
例 *tian*，的 第一声 有 子音字母 n, 其 第二声 就复写-*nn*=> *tiann*;
<u>第三声</u>：复写-*母音*同时复写-*nn*=> *tiaann*; <u>第四声</u>: 仅复写-*母音*=> *tiaan*.
<u>第六步</u>。加字母仿写的笔画或拼写部首后缀*** 来区别又同声又同调的单字, 例：
'甜'和'恬' =>'tiannjtd' 和 'tiannvlv'; 用 -jtd=舌 和 -vlv=忄后缀来分别同声字。
<u>第七步</u>。双音节连写方法:删掉部首后缀字母. 例：
妹+妹 => meeixx+meeixx =>meeimeei => 妹妹
<u>第八步</u>。三音节连写:删掉部首后缀字母，又同时删掉声调字母：
例：联+合+国 =>liannthht+hhejy+gguoq =>Liannhhegguo=> 联合国 =United Nations.
<u>第九步</u>。用CCC的PX2001导师学拼音+声调+首部就能按指法拼写汉字。
<u>第十步</u>。用CCC的拼音+拼写输入法系统用于视窗Windows，就能进入电脑中文世界！
*<u>注</u>：V H L J Y T G P C Z 是电脑世界的古老汉字十笔画的新名称:
Diaann, Henng, Shuu, Ppiee, Naa, Tti, Gou, Wan, Qu Zhhe也是书写各个世界形声字母的十笔画。
(备忘歌：Vvi维 He喝 Le了, Jii记 Yii忆 Tti提, Ggeei给 Penng朋 Ccai才 Zhi智!)
***部首后缀, buushhoou hoouzhuii, radical suffixes.
**[新华字典], Xinhhua Ziidiaann, Shangwuu Yinshuguan, 商务印书馆 1988,北京，中国

[A] INTERNET-CHINESE-ENGLISH TRILINGUAL DICTIONARETTE[4]

INTERNET-CHINESE	INTERNET-ENGLISH	CHINESE CHARACTERS
A a	[Linear Script]	[Square Script]
aanzhaao	according to	按照
anquann	safety	安全
Aolinpike [Aaolinnppiikee]	Olympic	Aolinpike 奥林匹克
Aolinpike [Aaolinnppiikee] Faandiaan	Olympic Hotel	奥林匹克饭店
B b	[Linear Script]	[Square Script]
baaozhhii	newspaper	报纸
Bbaaihuoo Daallou	Department Store	百货大楼
bbaaolleei	tower	堡垒
bbaifaan	white rice	白饭
Bbeeijing	Peking	北京
Bbeeijing Kkoouqiang Yiyuaan	Beijing Stomatology Hospital	北京 口腔 医院
Bbeeijing Xxiehhe Yiyuaan	Union Medical College Hospital	北京协和 医院
bbiaao xiongdii/jjieemeei	cousins	表兄弟/姐妹
bbiaaoyii ziiffu	ideograms	表意字符
bbie danxin	don't worry	别担心
bbie jieeyii	never mind	别介意
bbie zhhaojji	don't worry	别着急
bbowuuguaann	museum	博物 馆
biaozhuunnhuaa	standardization	标准化
biingle	sick	病了
buu anquannde	unsafe	不 安全的
buu doonng	don't understand	不懂
buu hhaao yiisi	embarrassed	不好意思
buu jjiuuj	not long	不久

[4] INTERNET-CHINESE-ENGLISH TRILINGUAL DICTIONARETTE, with its linguistic science and technology, forecasts a future dictionary, pointing to the direction of fully enhancing the current popular national standard, as a modernization reference: XINHUA DICTIONARY with English Translation, the Commercial Press International CO., LTD. Haan-Ying Shuangjjiee XINHHUA ZIIDIAANN, Shangwuu Yiinshuguaann Yyoouxiaan Gongsi; 汉-英双解-新华字典-商务印书馆有限公司 2001 -TSW 总 编译

INTERNET-CHINESE	INTERNET-ENGLISH	CHINESE CHARACTERS
buu yuaann	not far	不远
buu zhidaao jjieeshii	don't know	不知道
buunenng	cannot	不能
C c	*[Linear Script]*	*[Square Script]*
cai	guess	猜
caimmi yyouxii	guessing game	猜谜游戏
canguaann	restaurant	餐馆
canguan	visit	参观
canguan	sightsee	参观
channg an	long peace	长安
Channg Chenng	Great Wall	长城
Channg Chennghlt Faandiaan	Great Wall Hotel	长城饭店
channg shhijiaan	long time	长时间
Channgchenng	Great Wall	长城
che yyouvvt	car gas	车油
che zhhizhaao haaommaa	car license number	车执照号码
chenngkee	passengers	乘客
chenngshii	urban	乘势
chezhaan	station	车站
chhaodaai	dynasty	朝代
chhixuule zheeme jjiuuj	lasted so long	持续了这么久
chhouhuaa guanguang lleuuyyou	plan sightseeing tour	筹划观光旅游
chid yaaoh	take medicine	吃药
chou yanvk	smoke cigarette	抽烟
chunjuaann	egg roll	春卷
chuzuche	taxicab	出租车
cuimiann yaaohll	sleep medicine	催眠药
D d	*[Linear Script]*	*[Square Script]*
daa	big	大
daaibbiaao shennme?	stands for what?	代表甚么?
daanshii	but	但是

INTERNET-CHINESE	INTERNET-ENGLISH	CHINESE CHARACTERS
daaochuu	everywhere	到处
daaole	arrived	到了
daayi	coat	大意
danchenng	round trip	单程
dangrann	of course	当然
Darwin [Ddaeerrwenn]	Darwin	Darwin [达 尔 文]
ddaahuaaile	damaged	打坏了
deenng liaanng gee xxiaaoshhi	wait for two hours	等两个小时
deenng ninn	waiting for you	等您
deenng wwooj	wait for me	等我
diaanshii	television	电视
diaanyiinng	cinema	电影
diaaoyyu	fishing	钓鱼
diidiaann	site	地点
diidiaann	place	地点
diieer gee	the second one	第二个
diigguo zhonggguo	imperial china	帝国中国
diigguo-zhhuuyii	imperialism	帝国-主义
diigguo-zhhuuyiide riibeenn	imperialistic Japan	帝国-主义的日本
diitaann	carpets	地毯
diiyih shiijiee daazhaan	first world war	第一世界大战
dong an shiichaanng	tung-an market	东安市场
dong-dan yyoujju	dong-dan post office	东-单邮局
doongwuu yuannlph	zoological park	动物园
duiibuuqqii	sorry	对不起
duiide	correctly	对的
duiile	right	对了
duo daa	how big	多大
duo jjiuuh yyiiqiann	how long ago	多久以前
duo niann	many years ▯	多年
duo shhaao	how much	多少
duo xiee	many thanks	多谢

▦™ TiENSTROKES ® USA
www. internetchinese.com * China Certificate of Standardization®1999 * www.tienstrokes.com

INTERNET-CHINESE	INTERNET-ENGLISH	CHINESE CHARACTERS
duo yuaann	how far	多远
E e	[Linear Script]	[Square Script]
eehle	hungry	饿了
Eershhiyih Shiijii Faandiaan	Twenty-First Century Hotel	二十一世纪饭店
F f	[Linear Script]	[Square Script]
faandiaan	hotel	饭店
fangbiaan	convenient	方便
Fangkuaai Haanzii	Square Chinese	方块汉字
fannmanng jiaotong	heavy traffic	繁忙交通
feichanng	very	非常
feichanng gaannxiee	many thanks	非常感谢
feijichaanng	airport	飞机场
fengjiaan-zhiiduu	feudalism	封建-制度
fengshhuii	winds-waters [feng shui]	风水
fenzhong	minutes	分钟
Ffaagguo	France	法国
fuufeei	pay	付费
fuummuu	parents	父母
fuuqiann	pay	付钱
fuushhuu	subsidiary	附属
G g	[Linear Script]	[Square Script]
gaannjjue feichanng buu shufu	feel very sick	感觉非常不舒服
gaannmaao	flu	感冒
gaofeng shhijian	rush hours	高峰时间
gaoxiing bangmanng	glad to help	高兴帮忙
gaoxiingle	delighted	高兴了
gaozhong biiyee	high school graduate	高中毕业
geeng hhaao de zhhuuyii	better idea	更好的主义
ggaaishaan	improvement	改善
ggemiing	revolution	革命

INTERNET-CHINESE	INTERNET-ENGLISH	CHINESE CHARACTERS
gguojia	nation	国家
Gguojia Aolinpike Ttiiyuu Zhongxin	National Olympic Sports Center	国家 奥林匹克 体育 中心
gguojii	international	国际
Gguojii Faandiaan	International Hotel	国际饭店
Gguojii Juulee Buuvh	International Club, The	国际俱乐部
gguojii yilliaao zhongxin	international medical center	国际医疗中心
gongdiaan	palace	供电
gongllii	kilometers	公里
gongsi	corporation	公司
gongyiihz	arts and crafts	工艺
gongyuu	apartment	公寓
gooule	enough	够了
goouqiaang	time-pressed	够呛
guaanngchaanng	public square	广场
guaanngchaanng zaai nnaar	the square is where	广场在哪儿
guanguang	sightsee	观光
guanguangzhe	sight-seeing	观光着
guanzhuu	concentrate	关注
Guiibin Llou Faandiaan	Grand Hotel	贵宾楼饭店
guugong	palace	故宫
Guugong Bbowuu Guaannjpg	The Palace Museum	故宫博物馆
H h	*[Linear Script]*	*[Square Script]*
haaixiu	embarrassed	害羞
Haanyyuu Pinyin Ziimmuu	Chinese Language Phonetic Alphabet	汉语拼音字母
Haanzii	Chinese Characters	汉字
haaoqqide	curious	好奇的
halluo!	hello!	哈罗!
heenn daa	very big	很大

INTERNET-CHINESE	INTERNET-ENGLISH	CHINESE CHARACTERS
heenn duo tian	very many days	很多天
heenn guii	very expensive	很贵
heenn yuaann	very far	很远
hhaao zhhuuyii	good idea	好主义
hhaaode	good	好的
hhaaode minngtian	good tomorrow	好的明天
hhaiyyoou nnaar	else where	还有哪儿
hhaizi	children	孩子
hheguu	why so	何故
Hhepinng Binguaann	Peace Hotel	和平宾馆
hheshii	suitable	合适
hhuooche zhaan zaai nnaar	the train station is where	火车 在哪儿
hhuooche zhaanvh	railway station	火车站
hhuoyuee	dynamic	活跃
hhutoong	back alley	胡同
hhutoong	back streets	胡同
honngsee diitaann	red carpet	红色地毯
hooullai	after that	后来
huanngdii	emperor	皇帝
Huanngguan Jiaarii Faandiaan	Holiday Crown Plaza	皇冠假日饭店
huanyinng	welcome	欢迎
hunllii	wedding	婚礼
huoo	or	或
I i, J j	*[Linear Script]*	*[Square Script]*
jiaagge	prices	价格
jiaanng yidiaann yingwenn	speak a little English	讲一点英文
jiaanyii	advise	建议
jiaanyii	suggestions	建议
jiaaoshi	tutor	教师
jiaaotanng	church	教堂

⊞™ TiENSTROKES ® USA
www. internetchinese.com * China Certificate of Standardization®1999 * www.tienstrokes.com

INTERNET-CHINESE	INTERNET-ENGLISH	CHINESE CHARACTERS
jiaazhhi	worth	价值
Jiannadaa	Canada	加拿大
jiaotong	traffic	交通
jiayyou zhaan	gas station	加油站
jichaanng	airport	机场
jiedaao minngzi	street name	街道名字
jieeshaao	introduce	介绍
jiejiinzhe	approaching	接近着
jiichenngde	succeeding	继承的
jiijiaaqii	taximeter	记价器
jiinchu kkoou	import and export	进出口
jiiniaan	memorial	记念
jiiniaanbei	monument	记念碑
jiinruu	entrance	进入
jiixu kaiche	keep on driving	继续开车
jiizhuu	remember	记住
Jin Du Jiaarii Faandiaan	Holiday Inn Downtown	金都假日饭店
jingchanng	usually	经常
jinghuaa	mandarin	京话
jintian	today	今天
jjieeshii	explain	解释
jjiehunle	married	结婚了
Jjijiuu Diaanhuaa: 120	Emergency Phone: 120	急救电话: 120
Jiuujinshan	San Francisco	旧金山
junffa	warlords	军阀
junrenn	soldier	军人
juuchaanng	theater	剧场
K k	*[Linear Script]*	*[Square Script]*
kaan!	look!	看!
kaanllai hhai taai xinh	looks still too new	看来还太新
kaaojiin TianAnMenn	near Tiananmen (HeavenPeaceGate)	靠近天安门
kai che	drive car	开车

INTERNET-CHINESE	INTERNET-ENGLISH	CHINESE CHARACTERS
kai che zhe zzooule	driving car away	开车着走了
kai maanh yidiaann	drive slowly	开慢 一点
kai wannxiaao	kidding	开玩笑
kai wannxiaaodi	jokingly	开玩笑地
kaishhii	start	开始
keerenn	guest	客人
Kkaaoroou Yuaanq	Kaorou Wan Restaurant	烤肉园
Kkaaoya Diaanvhj	Duck Restaurant	烤鸭店
kkeeyyii	okay	可以
Koouzhuu Nniide Anquann Daaih	Buckle Your Safety Belt	扣 住 你的 安全带
kuaaihhuo	have fun	快活
Kunlunn Faandiaan	Kunlun Hotel	昆 仑 饭店
L l	*[Linear Script]*	*[Square Script]*
Liaang Mmaa Faandiaan	Landmark Hotel	亮马饭店
liannxuuxiing	continuity	连续 性
Liidu Jiaarii Faandiaan	Holiday Inn Lido	丽 都 假日饭店
liingwaaide luu	another road	另外的 路
liishhii keechenng	history lesson	历史 课程
liivh yigee zhaanghaao	open an account	立 一个 帐号
llaaobaann	boss	老板
lleuuguaann	hotels	旅馆
lleuuxinngshe	travel service	旅行社
lliaao buuqqii!	impressive!	了不起!
lliipiinn	gift	礼品
lliuliidi	fluently	流利地
LluGouQqiao	Marco Polo Bridge	卢沟桥
luu	street	路
M m	*[Linear Script]*	*[Square Script]*
maaoyii	business	贸易
maaoyii	trade	贸易
Mennggguu	Mongol	蒙 古
miimii	secret	密秘

INTERNET-CHINESE	INTERNET-ENGLISH	CHINESE CHARACTERS
Minng Huanngdii	Ming Emperor	明皇帝
Minng Linng	Ming Tombs	明陵
minngtian	tomorrow	明天
minngtian kkeeyyii ma?	tomorrow okay	明天可以吗？
minngzi	name	名字
minnzzu	nation	民族
Minnzzu Min Tzu Faandiaan	Nationalities Hotel	民族饭店
minnzzude	national	民族的
mmafann ninn	trouble you	麻烦您
mmao	hair	毛
Mmao Zzevvt Dong	Mao Zedong	毛泽东
mmaobiing	illness	毛病
Mmeeishuu Guaannjpg	Art Gallery	美术馆
Mmeeigguo	America	美国
Mmeeigguo Yingwenn	American English	美国英文
mmeeigguorenn	Americans	美国人
mmeeijin	dollars	美金
mmeeiliide	beautiful	美丽的
mmeeitian	everyday	每天
mmei guanxi	no problem	没关系
mmei shennme	don't mention	没甚么
mmei shiih	no matter	没事
mmeiyyoou shhijian	no time	没有时间
N n	*[Linear Script]*	*[Square Script]*
naame	then	那么
nannhhai	boy	男孩
neei zhaan	civil war	内战
nenng	can	能
ninn shou xiaa linngqiann	you keep the change	您收下零钱
ninn zhen hhaao	very kind of you	您真好
nna hhaao shoujuu	keep the receipt	拿好收据
nnaa cenng llou	which floor	哪层楼

INTERNET-CHINESE	INTERNET-ENGLISH	CHINESE CHARACTERS
nnaa niann	what year	哪年
nnaa shii shennme	what is that	哪是甚么
nnaar	where	哪儿
nneuuhhai	girl	女孩
NneuuHuanng Ccixxii	Empress Dowager Cixi	女皇慈禧
nniaao	bird	鸟
nniaao yaann guanguang!	bird's eye view!	鸟眼观光!
nnii yaao kongttiao ma?	do you want air-conditioning	你要 空调吗？
nniide	your	你的
nniide jiaanyii	your suggestions	你的 建议
nnii hhaao!	you well!	你 好!
nniij xxiihuan	you like	你 喜欢
O o; P p	*[Linear Script]*	*[Square Script]*
penngyyoou	friends	朋友
Penshee-Feiji Shhicha Biingzheeng	Jet Lag Syndrome	喷射-飞机时差 病 症
Pinxxiee Ziimmuu	Pinxxiee Alphabet	拼写 字母
Pinyin Ziimmuu	Pinyin Alphabet	拼音字母
Ppuutonghuaa	General Speech [Putonghua]	普通话
Q q	*[Linear Script]*	*[Square Script]*
qiinng	please	请
qingzhensii	mosque	清真寺
qinluee zhhee	invaders	侵略 者
qinqi	relatives	亲戚
qizi	wife	妻子
qqiaoh	bridge	桥
qqiichuanng	get up	起床
qqiifa wwooj	enlighten me	启发我
qqiyiide	fantastic	棋艺的
qqizhii	flags	旗帜

⊞ ™ TiENSTROKES ® USA

www. internetchinese.com * China Certificate of Standardization®1999 * www.tienstrokes.com

INTERNET-CHINESE	INTERNET-ENGLISH	CHINESE CHARACTERS
quannqqiu-xiingde weentti	globalization problem	全球性的问题
quu nnaar	to where	去哪儿
Quu ZhongGguo Yinnhanng	To Bank Of China	去中国银行
R r	[Linear Script]	[Square Script]
Rennminn Daahuii Tanng	Great Hall of the People	人民大会堂
Rennminn Jjieefaang Jun	People's Liberation Army	人民 解放 军
Rennminn Yingxionng Jiiniaanbei	The Peoples Heroes Monument	人民 英雄 记念碑
ronngxiing	proud	荣幸
rrugguoo	if	如果
rruhhe	how	如何
S s	[Linear Script]	[Square Script]
shaang che	get in car	上车
shaang xxue	go to school	上学
shangdiaan & canting	shops & restaurants	商店＆餐厅
shaoh deenng	wait a moment	稍 等
sheenng shhijian	save time	省时间
shengde	born	生的
shenkeede jiinngsee!	impressive view!	深刻的景色!
shennme	what	甚么
shennme diifang	which place	甚么地方
shennme shhihoou	what time	甚么时候
shennme shii	what is	甚么是
shennme yiisi	what sense	甚么意思
shensizhe	deep in thought	深思着
shhei	who	谁
shhi fenzhong	ten minutes	十分钟
shhijian goou ma?	is that enough time?	时间够吗？
Shhisan [Dii-13] Shiijii	Thirteenth [13th] Century	十三 [第 -13] 世纪
shhoottibao	handbag	手提包
shhooudu	capital	首都

INTERNET-CHINESE	INTERNET-ENGLISH	CHINESE CHARACTERS
shii zheeyaang	is that right	是这样吗？
shiide	yes	是的
shiijii	century	世纪
ShoouPiaao Chuu	Booking Office	售票处
shu	books	书
shudiaan	bookstores	书店
shuiide hhaao	slept well	睡的好
shuo	say	说
siimiaao	temple	寺庙
siimiaao & jiaaotanng	temples & churches	寺庙&教堂
siwwei	thought	思维
suanlaa tang	hot-&-sour soup	酸辣汤
suuduu xiaanzhhii	speed limit	速度限止
T t	*[Linear Script]*	*[Square Script]*
taai waannle	too late	太晚了
takeesi	taxi	他客司
tamen gaanle shennme	they did what?	他们干了甚么
tamen shii shhei	they were who	他们是谁?
tanng	hall	堂
tannghuanng	imposing	堂皇
tanntian	chats	谈天
teebbie hhaao	specially good	特别好
tian	heaven	天
Tian An Menn	Heaven Peace Gate	天安门
Tian An Menn De Qiannmiaan	TianAnMen's Front	天安门的前面
Tian An Menn Guaanngchaanng	TianAnMen Square	天安门广场
Tian Lunn Wanngchhao Faandiaan	Tianlun Dynasty Hotel	天仑王朝饭店
tianshaangde	celestial	天上的
tianshhiide	angelic	天使的
Tiantann	Temple Of Heaven	天坛

▦™ TiENSTROKES ® USA
www. internetchinese.com * China Certificate of Standardization®1999 * www.tienstrokes.com

INTERNET-CHINESE	INTERNET-ENGLISH	CHINESE CHARACTERS
Tianzhhuu Jiaaotanng	Catholic Church	天主教堂
tingle haaoqqi	sounds intriguing	听了好奇
tinng che	*parking the car*	停车
tinng zaai	stop at	停在
tonngyii	agree	同意
toonngyihuaa	unification	统一化
ttiicao	exercise	体操
ttixiinng wwooj	remind me	提醒我
ttoutoong	headache	头痛
ttuzhong	on the way	途中
U u; V v; W w	*[Linear Script]*	*[Square Script]*
waaijiao	diplomacy	外交
waaijiaojia	diplomat	外交家
waaillai	foreign	外来
waaimaao	foreign trade	外贸
Waaiwenn Chubaann Shee	Foreign Languages Press	外文出版社
waann an	good night	晚安
Wanng Ffuuvhj Jiinng	King's Palace Courtyard	王府井
Wannjuu Buuvhvjh	Toy Department	玩具部
weeishennme	why	为甚么
weentti	questions	问题
wennhuaa	culture	文化
WooFfoSii	The Temple Of Reclining Buddha	卧佛寺
wuraann	pollution	污染
wwoo	I	我
wwooj	I	我
wwoo buucuoo	I am fine	我不错
wwoo gaoxiing wwei ninn ffuwuu	I am glad to serve you	我高兴为您服务
wwoo minngbbai	I see	我明白
wwoode	my	我的

INTERNET-CHINESE	INTERNET-ENGLISH	CHINESE CHARACTERS
wwoode shengjii	my livelihood	我的生计
wwooj gaoxiing	my pleasure	我高兴
wwooj jiizhuu naagee	I remember that	我记住那个
wwooj xiangxiin kkeeyyii	I believe so	我 相信可以
wwooj zaai kaan	I am looking	我在看
wwoomen daaole	here we have arrived	我们到了
wwuu-sii yuundoong	may 4th movement	五-四运动
X x	*[Linear Script]*	*[Square Script]*
xiaang yoouh	left	向右
xiaang zzuooh	right	向左
xiaanngxiaang	imagine	想像
xiaaozhe	*laughing*	笑着
Xiaatian	**Summer**	夏天
Xiang Shan Faandiaan	**Hsiang Shan Hotel**	香山饭店
xiansheng	mister	先生
xianzaai	now	现在
xiarenn jjiaaozi	shrimp dumplings	虾仁饺子
xieexiee	thanks	谢谢
xifangde	western	西方的
xiih hhaao nniide anquann daaih	fasten your seat belt	系好你的安全带
xiinyoong kkaa	credit card	信用卡
xinde	new	新
xinde shiijiee	new world	新的世界
Xinhhua Xinwennshee	**New China News Agency**	新华新闻社
xinngshiih	norm	形式
xinwenn-jiizhhee	journalist	新闻-记者
xiwaang	hope	希望
xuyaao bangmanng	need help	需要帮忙
xxieede	written	写的
xxiihuan	enjoy	喜欢
xxuede	learned	学的
Y y	*[Linear Script]*	*[Square Script]*

⊞™ TiENSTROKES ® USA
www. internetchinese.com * China Certificate of Standardization®1999 * www.tienstrokes.com

INTERNET-CHINESE	INTERNET-ENGLISH	CHINESE CHARACTERS
yaao	want	要
yidiaann	a little	一点
yih eer san sii wwuuh …	one two three four five…	一二三四五…
yih zzaao	next morning	一早
yilliao zhongxin	clinic center	医疗中心
Yinggguo	England	英国
Yingllii	English Miles	英里
yingmmuu	acres	英亩
Yingwenn Ziimmuu	English Alphabet	英文字母
yingxionng	heroes	英雄
Yingyyuu	English	英语
yinnhanng	bank	银行
Yinnhanng, Zhonggguo	Bank Of China	银行,中国
yishengh	doctor	医生
yiyuaan	hospital	医院
yoong diaanti	use elevator	用电梯
yoong xiyih	western medicine	用西医
yoouzhiiyuann	kindergarten	幼稚园
yuannliaang	pardon	原谅
Yyihhe Yuann	Summer Palace	颐和园
yyoou yih tian	there is one day	有一天
yyoouminngde diifang	famous places	有名的地方
Yyoouyii Faandiaan	Friendship Hotel	友谊饭店
Yyoouyii Shangdiaan	Friendship Store	友谊商店
yyoulaann	visiting	游览
Yyukuaai Lleuuttu!	Happy Trip!	愉快旅途!
Z z	*[Linear Script]*	*[Square Script]*
zaai wwuufaan hoou	after lunch	在午饭后
zaai yooubian	on the right	在右边
zaai zzuoobian	on the left	在左边
zaaiijiaan	see you again	再见
zeennme ggaaibiaanle?	how changed?	怎么改变了?
zhaannlaann	exhibition	展览

INTERNET-CHINESE	INTERNET-ENGLISH	CHINESE CHARACTERS
zhaaoxiaangji	camera	照相机
zhaaoxiaang-xinwenn jiizhhee	photo-journalist	照相-新闻记者
zhao	morning	朝
zhaodaai yaanhuii	reception feast	招待宴会
zhee	this	这
zhee jiuuvh shii	this is it	这就是
zhee shii	this is	这是
zhee shii buu pinngchanng	this is not usual	这是不平常
zhee shii shennme	what is this	这是甚么
zheellii buu xxuu tinngche	parking is not allowed here	这里不许停车
zheeme jiin	so near	这么近
zheeng zaai zheer!	right here!	正在这儿!
zheengminngshu	certificate	证明书
zheengzhii jiihuaa	political project	政治计划
zhen buucuoo	that's great	真不错
zhenchenngdi	seriously	真诚地
zhende	indeed	真的
zhenssuoo	clinic	诊所
zhhaaodaao le	found it	找到了
zhhujiaandi	gradually	逐渐地
zhhuuxxi	chairman	主席
zhhuuyii	idea [-ism]	主义
Zhong Yihc	Chinese Medicine	中医
ZhongGguo	China	中国
Zhonggguo Minnhanng Zoonngjju	CAAC	中国民航总局
ZhongGguo Wwawwa	China Dolls	中国娃娃
Zhonghhua Rennminn Goonghhegguo	Peoples Republic Of China	中华人民共和国
Zhongshan Gongyuannjl	Chungshan Park	中山公园
zhongttou	hour	钟头

INTERNET-CHINESE	INTERNET-ENGLISH	CHINESE CHARACTERS
zhongxxue biiyee	middle school graduate	中学 毕业
zhuanjia	professional	专家
zhuuminngde	famous	著名
zhuunnbeei zzoou	readying to go	准备走
Ziiyyou Shiichaanng	Free Markets	自由市场
ziizun xin	self-regard	自尊心
zonghhehuaa	integration	综合化
zongjiaao	religion	宗教
zoonngbuu	head-office	总部
zuiihhaaode daaiyuu	best deal	最好的待遇
zzaao	morning	早
zzaaofaan	breakfast	早饭
zzugoou	enough	足够

⊞™ TIENSTROKES ® USA
www. internetchinese.com * China Certificate of Standardization®1999 * www.tienstrokes.com

[B] INTERNET-ENGLISH-CHINESE TRILINGUAL DICTIONARETTE

INTERNET-ENGLISH	INTERNET-CHINESE	CHINESE CHARACTERS
A a	*[Linear Script]*	*[Square Script]*
a little	yidiaann	一点
according to	aanzhaao	按照
acres	yingmmuu	英亩
advise	jiaanyii	建议
after lunch	zaai wwuufaan hoou	在午饭后
after that	hooullai	后来
agree	tonngyii	同意
airport	jichaanng	机场
America	Mmeeigguo	美国
American English	Mmeeigguo Yingwenn	美国英文
Americans	Mmeeigguorenn	美国人
angelic	tianshhiide	天使的
another road	liingwaaide luu	另外的路
apartment	gongyuu	公寓
approaching	jiejiinzhe	接近着
arrived	daaole	到了
Art Gallery	Mmeeishuu Guaannjpg	美术馆
arts and crafts	gongyiihz	工艺
B b	*[Linear Script]*	*[Square Script]*
back streets	hhutoong	胡同
bank	yinnhanng	银行
Bank of China	Yinnhanng, Zhonggguo	银行,中国
beautiful	mmeeiliide	美丽的
Beijing Stomatology Hospital	Bbeeijing Kkoouqiang Yiyuaan	北京口腔医院
best deal	zuiihhaaode daaiyuu	最好的待遇
better idea	geeng hhaao de zhhuuyii	更好的主义
big	daa	大
bird	nniaao	鸟
bird's eye view!	nniaao yaann guanguang!	鸟眼观光!

INTERNET-ENGLISH	INTERNET-CHINESE	CHINESE CHARACTERS
Booking Office	ShoouPiaao Chuu	售票处
books	shu	书
bookstores	shudiaan	书店
born	shengde	生的
boy	nannhhai	男孩
breakfast	zzaaofaan	早饭
bridge	qqiaoh	桥
Buckle Your Safety Belt	Koouzhuu Nniide Anquann Daaih	扣住 你的 安全 带
business	maaoyii	贸易
but	daanshii	但是
C c	*[Linear Script]*	*[Square Script]*
CAAC	ZhongGguo Minnhanng Zoonngjju	中国 民航 总局
camera	zhaaoxiaangji	照相机
can	nenng	能
Canada	Jiannadaa	加拿大
cannot	buunenng	不能
capital	shhooudu	首都
car gas	che yyouvvt	车油
car license number	che zhhizhaao haaommaa	车执照号码
carpets	diitaann	地毯
Catholic Church	Tianzhhuu Jiaaotanng	天主教堂
celestial	tiande	天的
century	shiijii	世纪
certificate	zheengminngshu	证明书
chairman	zhhuuxxi	主席
chats	tanntian	谈天
children	hhaizi	孩子
China	ZhongGguo	中国
China Dolls	ZhongGguo Wwawwa	中国娃娃
Chinese Characters	Haanzii	汉字

INTERNET-ENGLISH	INTERNET-CHINESE	CHINESE CHARACTERS
Chinese Language Phonetic Alphabet	Haanyyuu Pinyin Ziimmuu	汉语拼音字母
Chinese Medicine	Zhong Yihc	中医
Chungshan Park	Zhongshan Gongyuannjl	中山公园
church	jiaaotanng	教堂
cinema	diaanyiinng	电影
civil war	neei zhaan	内战
clinic	zhenssuoo	诊所
clinic center	yilliao zhongxin	医疗中心
coat	daayi	大意
concentrate	guanzhuu	关注
continuity	liannxuuxiing	连续性
convenient	fangbiaan	方便
corporation	gongsi	公司
correct	duiide	对的
cousins	bbiaao xiongdii/ jjieemeei	表兄弟/姐妹
credit card	xiinyoong kkaa	信用卡
culture	wennhuaa	文化
curious	haaoqqide	好奇的
D d	*[Linear Script]*	*[Square Script]*
damaged	ddaahuaaile	打坏了
Darwin	Darwin [Ddaeerrwenn]	**Darwin** [达尔文]
deep in thought	shensizhe	深思着
delighted	gaoxiingle	高兴了
department store	bbaaihuoo daallou	百货大楼
diplomat	waaijiaojia	外交家
diplomatic	waaijiao	外交
do you want air-conditioning?	nnii yaao kongttiao ma?	你要空调吗？
doctor	yishengh	医生
dollar	mmeeijin	美金
don't mention	mmei shennme	没甚么
don't know	buu zhidaao	不知道

▦™ TiENSTROKES ® USA
www. internetchinese.com * China Certificate of Standardization®1999 * www.tienstrokes.com

INTERNET-ENGLISH	INTERNET-CHINESE	CHINESE CHARACTERS
don't understand	buu doonng	不懂
don't worry	bbie danxin	别担心
don't worry	bbie zhhaojji	别着急
Dong-Dan Post Office	Dong-Dan Yyoujju	东-单邮局
drive car	kaiche	开车
drive slowly	kai maanh yidiaann	开慢 一点
driving away	kaichezhe zzooule	开车着走了
Duck Restaurant	Kkaaoya Diaanvhj	烤鸭店
dynamic	hhuoyuee	活跃
dynasty	chhaodaai	朝代
E e	*[Linear Script]*	*[Square Script]*
egg roll	chunjuaann	春卷
else where	hhaiyyoou nnaar	还有哪儿
embarrassed	buu hhaao yiisi	不好意思
embarrassed	haaixiu	害羞
Emergency Phone: 120	Jjijiuu Diaanhuaa: 120	急救 电话: 120
emperor	huanngdii	皇帝
Empress Dowager Cixi	NneuuHuanng Ccixxii	女皇慈禧
England	Yinggguo	英国
English Alphabet	Yingwenn Ziimmuu	英文字母
English Miles	Yingllii	英里
English speech	Yingyyuu	英语
enjoy	xxiihuan	喜欢
enlighten me	qqiifa wwooj	启发我
enough	gooule	够了
enough	zzugoou	足够
entrance	jiinruu	进入
everyday	mmeeitian	每天
everywhere	daaochuu	到处
exercise	ttiicao	体操
exhibition	zhaannlaann	展览
explain	jjieeshii	解释
F f	*[Linear Script]*	*[Square Script]*

INTERNET-ENGLISH	INTERNET-CHINESE	CHINESE CHARACTERS
famous	zhuuminngde	著名的
famous places	yyoouminngde diifang	有名的地方
fantastic	qqiyiide	奇异的
fasten your seat belt	xiih hhaao nniide anquann daaih	系好你的安全带
feel very sick	gaannjjue feichanng buu shufu	感觉非常不舒服
feudalism	fengjiaan-zhiiduu	封建-制度
First World War	Diiyih Shiijiee Daa zhaan	第一世界大战
fishing	diaaoyyu	钓鱼
flags	qqizhii	旗帜
flu	gaannmaao	感冒
fluently	lliuliidi	流利地
foreign	waaillai	外来
Foreign Languages Press	Waaiwenn Chubaann Shee	外文出版社
foreign trade	waaimaao	外贸
found it	zhhaaodaao le	找到了
France	Ffaagguo	法国
Free Markets	Ziiyyou Shiichaanng	自由市场
friends	penngyyoou	朋友
Friendship Hotel	Yyoouyii Faandiaan	友谊饭店
Friendship Store	Yyoouyii Shangdiaan	友谊商店
G g	*[Linear Script]*	*[Square Script]*
gas station	jiayyou zhaan	加油展
General Speech [Putonghua]	Ppuutonghuaa	普通化
get in car	shaang che	上车
get up	qqiichuanng	起床
gift	lliipiinn	礼品
girl	nneuuhhai	女孩
glad to help	gaoxiing bangmanng	高兴帮忙

INTERNET-ENGLISH	INTERNET-CHINESE	CHINESE CHARACTERS
global problem	quannqqiu-xiingde weentti	全球性的问题
go to school	shaang xxue	上学
good	hhaaode	好的
good idea	hhaao zhhuuyii	好主义
good night	waann an	晚安
good tomorrow	hhaaode minngtian	好的明天
got a light	mmei guanxi qinng ba	没关系
gradually	zhhujiaandi	逐渐地
Grand Hotel	Guiibin Llou Faandiaan	贵宾楼饭店
Great Hall Of The People	Rennminn Daahuii Tanng	人民大会堂
Great Wall	Channg ChennghIt	长城
Great Wall	ChanngChenng	长城
Great Wall Hotel	ChanngChenng Faandiaan	长城饭店
guess	cai	猜
guessing game	caimmi yyouxii	猜谜游戏
guest	keerenn	客人
H h	**[Linear Script]**	**[Square Script]**
hair	mmao	毛
hall	tanng	堂
handbag	shhoottibao	手提包
Happy Trip!	Yyukuaai Lleuuttu!	愉快旅途!
have fun	kuaaihhuo	快活
headache	ttoutoong	头痛
head-office	zoonngbuu	总部
heaven	tian	天
Heavenly Peace Gate	Tian An Menn	天安门
heavy traffic	fannmanng jiaotong	繁忙交通
hello!	halluo!	哈罗!
here we have arrived	wwoomen daaole	我们到了
heroes	yingxionng	英雄
hhutoong	back alley	胡同

INTERNET-ENGLISH	INTERNET-CHINESE	CHINESE CHARACTERS
high school graduate	gaozhong biiyee	高中毕业
history lesson	liishhii keechenng	历史 课程
Holiday Crown Plaza	Huanngguan Jiaarii Faandiaan	皇冠假日饭店
Holiday Inn Downtown	Jin Du Jiaarii Faandiaan	金都假日饭店
Holiday Inn Lido	Liidu Jiaarii Faandiaan	丽都假日饭店
hope	xiwaang	希望
hospital	yiyuaan	医院
hot-&-sour soup	suanlaa tang	酸辣汤
hotel	faandiaan	饭店
hotels	lleuuguaann	旅馆
hour	zhongttou	钟头
how	rruhhe	如何
how big	duo daa	多大
how changed?	zeennme ggaaibiaanle?	怎么 改变了?
how far	duo yuaann	多远
how is that	hhaaode	好的
how long ago	duo jjiuuh yyiiqiann	多久 以前
how much	duo shhaao	多少
Hsiang Shan Hotel	Xiang Shan Faandiaan	香山饭店
hungry	eehle	饿了
I i	*[Linear Script]*	*[Square Script]*
I	wwoo	我
I am fine	wwoo buucuoo	我不错
I am glad to serve you	wwoo gaoxiing wwei ninn ffuwuu	我高兴为您服务
I am looking	wwooj zaai kaan	我在看
I believe so	wwooj xiangxiin kkeeyyii	我 相信可以
I remember that	wwooj jiizhuu naagee	我记住那个
I see	wwoo minngbbai	我明白
idea [-ism]	zhhuuyii	主义
ideograms	bbiaaoyii ziiffu	表意字符
if	rrugguoo	如果

⊞™ TiENSTROKES ® USA
www. internetchinese.com * China Certificate of Standardization®1999 * www.tienstrokes.com

INTERNET-ENGLISH	INTERNET-CHINESE	CHINESE CHARACTERS
illness	mmaobiing	毛病
imagine	xiaanngxiaang	想像
imperial china	diigguo zhonggguo	帝国中国
imperialism	diigguo-zhhuuyii	帝国-主义
imperialistic Japan	diigguo-zhhuuyiide riibeenn	帝国-主义的日本
import and export	jiinchu kkoou	进出口
imposing	tannghuanng	堂皇
impressive view!	shenkeede jiinngsee!	深刻的景色!
impressive!	lliaao buuqqii!	了不起!
improvement	ggaaishaan	改善
indeed	zhende	真的
integration	zonghhehuaa	综合化
international	gguojii	国际
International Club, The	Gguojii Juulee Buuvh	国际俱乐部
International Hotel	Gguojii Faandiaan	国际饭店
international medical center	gguojii yilliaao zhongxin	国际医疗中心
introduce	jieeshaao	介绍
invaders	qinluee zhhee	侵略者
is this right?	shii zhee yaang ma?	是这样吗?
J j	*[Linear Script]*	*[Square Script]*
Jet Lag Syndrome	Penshee-Feiji Shhicha Biingzheeng	喷射-飞机时差病症
jokingly	kaiwannxiaaodi	开玩笑地
journalist	xinwenn-jiizhhee	新闻-记者
K k	*[Linear Script]*	*[Square Script]*
Kaorou Wan Restaurant	Kkaaoroou Yuaanq	烤肉园
keep on driving	jiixu kaiche	继续开车
keep the receipt	nna hhaao shoujuu	拿好收据
kidding	kai wannxiaaodi	开玩笑
kilometers	gongllii	公里
kindergarten	yoouzhiiyuann	幼稚园

INTERNET-ENGLISH	INTERNET-CHINESE	CHINESE CHARACTERS
Kunlun Hotel	Kunlunn Faandiaan	昆仑饭店
L l	*[Linear Script]*	*[Square Script]*
Landmark Hotel	Liaang Mmaa Faandiaan	亮马饭店
lasted so long	chhixuule zheeme jjiuuj	持续了这么久
laughing	xiaaozhe	笑着
learned	xxuede	学的
left	xiaang yoouh	向右
long peace	channg an	长安
long time	channg shhijiaan	长时间
look!	kaan!	看!
looks still too new	kaanllai hhai taai xinh	看来还太新
M m	*[Linear Script]*	*[Square Script]*
manager	llaaobaann	老板
Mandarin	Jinghuaa	京话
many thanks	duo xiee	多谢
many thanks	feichanng gaannxiee	非常感谢
many years ▯	duo niann	多年
Mao Zedong	Mmao Zzevvt Dong	毛泽东
Marco Polo Bridge	LluGouQqiao	卢沟桥
married	jjiehunle	结婚了
may 4th movement	wwuu-sii yuundoong	五-四运动
memorial	jiiniaan	记念
middle school graduate	zhongxxue biiyee	中学毕业
Ming Emperor	Minng Huanngdii	明皇帝
Ming Tombs	Minng Linng	明陵
minutes	fenzhong	分钟
mister	xiansheng	先生
Mongol	Mennggguu	蒙古
monument	jiiniaanbei	记念碑
morning	zhao	朝
morning	zzaao	早
mosque	qingzhen siith	清真寺
museum	bbowuuguaann	博物馆

INTERNET-ENGLISH	INTERNET-CHINESE	CHINESE CHARACTERS
my	wwoode	我的
my livelihood	wwoode shengjii	我的生计
my pleasure	wwooj gaoxiing	我高兴
N n	*[Linear Script]*	*[Square Script]*
name	minngzi	名字
nation	gguojia	国家
nation	minnzzu	民族
national	minnzzude	民族的
National Olympic Sports Center	Gguojia Aolinpike Ttiiyuu Zhongxin	国家奥林匹克体育中心
Nationalities Hotel	Minnzzu (Min Tzu) Faandiaan	民族饭店
Near Tian An Men	Kaaojiin Tian An Menn	靠近天安门
need help	xuyaao bangmanng	需要帮忙
never mind	bbie jieeyii	别介意
new	xinde	新的
New China News Agency	Xinhhua Xinwennshee	新华新闻社
new world	xinde shiijiee	新的世界
newspaper	baaozhhii	报纸
next morning	yih zzaao	一早
no problem	mmei shiih	没事
no time	mmeiyyoou shhijian	没有时间
norm	xinngshiijv	形式
not far	buu yuaann	不远
not long	buu jjiuuj	不久
now	xianzaai	现在
O o	*[Linear Script]*	*[Square Script]*
of course	dangrann	当然
okay	kkeeyyii	可以
Olympic	Aaolinnppiikee [Aolinpike]	奥林匹克 (Aolinpike)
Olympic Hotel	Aaolinnppiikee [Aolinpike] Faandiaan	奥林匹克 (Aolinpike) 饭店
on the left	zaai zzuoobian	在左边

INTERNET-ENGLISH	INTERNET-CHINESE	CHINESE CHARACTERS
on the right	zaai yooubian	在右边
on the way	ttuzhong	途中
one two three four five...	yih eer san sii wwuuh ...	一二三四五 ...
open an account	liivh yigee zhaanghaao	立一个帐号
or	huoo	或
P p	*[Linear Script]*	*[Square Script]*
palace	gongdiaan	供电
palace	guugong	故宫
Palace Museum, The	Guugong Bbowuu Guaannjpg	故宫博物馆
pardon	yuannliaang	原谅
parents live in	fuummuu	父母
parking is not allowed here	zheellii buu xxuu tinngche	这里不许停车
parking the car	tinng che	停车
passengers	chenngkee	乘客
pay	fuufeei	付费
pay	fuuqiann	付钱
Peace Hotel	Hhepinng Binguaann	和平宾馆
Peking	Bbeeijing	北京
People's Liberation Army	Rennminn Jjieefaang Jun	人民解放军
Peoples Heroes Monument	Rennminn Yingxionng Jiiniaanbei	人民英雄记念碑
Peoples Republic Of China	Zhonghhua Rennminn Goonghhegguo	中华人民共和国
photo journalist	zhaaoxiaang-xinwenn jiizhhee	照相-新闻记者
Pinxxiee Alphabet	Pinxxiee Ziimmuu	拼写字母
Pinyin Alphabet	Pinyin Ziimmuu	拼音字母
place	diidiaann	地点
plan sightseeing tour	chhouhuaa guanguang lleuuyyou	筹划观光旅游
please	qiinng	请

☷ ™ TiENSTROKES ® USA
www.internetchinese.com * China Certificate of Standardization®1999 * www.tienstrokes.com

INTERNET-ENGLISH	INTERNET-CHINESE	CHINESE CHARACTERS
political project	zheengzhii jiihuaa	政治计划
pollution	wuraann	污染
prices	jiaagge	价格
professional	zhuanjia	专家
proud	ronngxiing	荣幸
public square	guaanngchaanng	广场
Q q	*[Linear Script]*	*[Square Script]*
questions	weentti	问题
R r	*[Linear Script]*	*[Square Script]*
railway station	hhuooche zhaanvh	火车站
readying to go	zhuunnbeei zzoou	准备走
reception feast	zhaodaai yaanhuii	招待宴会
Reclining Buddha Temple	WooFfoSii	卧佛寺
red carpet	honngsee diitaann	红色地毯
relatives	qinqi	亲戚
religion	zongjiaao	宗教
remember	jiizhuu	记住
remind me	ttixiinng wwooj	提醒我
restaurant	canguaann	餐馆
revolution	ggemiing	革命
right	duiile	对了
right	xiaang zzuooh	向左
right here!	zheeng zaai zheer!	正在这儿!
round trip	danchenng	单程
rush hours	gaofeng shhijian	高峰时间
S s	*[Linear Script]*	*[Square Script]*
safety	anquann	安全
San Francisco	Jjiuujinshan	旧金山
say	shuo	说
second one	diieer gee	第二个
secret	miimii	密秘
see you again	zaaiijiaan	再见

田™ TiENSTROKES ® USA

www.internetchinese.com * China Certificate of Standardization®1999 * www.tienstrokes.com

INTERNET-ENGLISH	INTERNET-CHINESE	CHINESE CHARACTERS
self-regard	ziizun xin	自尊心
seriously	zhenchenngdi	真诚地
shops & restaurants	shangdiaan & canting	商店＆餐厅
shrimp dumplings	xiarenn jjiaaozi	虾仁饺子
sick	biingle	病了
sightsee	canguan	参观
sightsee	guanguang	观光
sight-seeing	guanguangzhe	观光着
site	diidiaann	地点
sleep medicine	cuimiann yaaohll	催眠药
slept well	shuiide hhaao	睡的好
smoke cigarette	chou yanvk	抽烟
so near	zheeme jiin	这么近
soldier	junrenn	军人
sorry	duiibuuqqii	对不起
sounds intriguing	tingle haaoqqi	听了好奇
speak a little English	jiaanng yidiaann Yingwenn	讲一点英文
specially good	teebbie hhaao	特别好
speed limit	suuduu xiaanzhhii	速度限止
Square Chinese Characters	Fangkuaai Haanvvt Ziivvp	方块汉字
square is where	guaanngchaanng zaai nnaar	广场在哪儿
standardization	biaozhuunnhuaa	标准化
stands for what?	daaibbiaao shennme?	代表甚么?
start	kaishhii	开始
station	chezhaan	车站
stop at	tinng zaai	停在
street	luu	路
street name	jiedaao minngzi	街道名字
subsidiary	fuushhuu	附属
succeeding	jiichenngde	继承的
suggestions	jiaanyii	建议

田™ TiENSTROKES ® USA
www. internetchinese.com * China Certificate of Standardization®1999 * www.tienstrokes.com

INTERNET-ENGLISH	INTERNET-CHINESE	CHINESE CHARACTERS
suitable	hheshii	合适
Summer	Xiaatian	夏天
Summer Palace	Yyihhe Yuannlph	颐和园
T t	*[Linear Script]*	*[Square Script]*
take medicine	chid yaaoh	吃药
take the elevator	yoong diaanti	用电梯
taxi	takeesi	他客司
taxicab	chuzuche	出租车
taximeter	jiijiaaqii	记价器
television	diaanshii	电视
temple	siimiaao	寺庙
Temple Of Heaven	Tiantann	天坛
temples & churches	siimiaao & jiaaotanng	寺庙＆教堂
ten minutes	shhi fenzhong	十分钟
thanks	xieexiee	谢谢
that enough time	shhijian goou	时间够吗？
that's great	zhen buucuoo	真不错
theater	juuchaanng	剧场
then	naame	那么
there is one day	yyoou yih tian	有一天
they did what?	tamen gaanle shennme	他们干了甚么
they were who	tamen shii shhei	他们是谁?
Thirteenth [13th] Century	Shhisan [Dii-13] Shiijii	十三 [第 -13] 世纪
this	zhee	这
this is	zhee shii	这是
this is it	zhee jiuuvh shii	这就是
this is not usual	zhee shii buu pinngchanng	这是不平常
thought	siwwei	思维
TianAnMen Square	Tian An Menn Guaanngchaanng	天安门广场
TianAnMen's Front	Tian An Menn De Qiannmiaan	天安门的前面

INTERNET-ENGLISH	INTERNET-CHINESE	CHINESE CHARACTERS
Tianlun Dynasty Hotel	Tian Lunn Wanngchhao Faandiaan	天仑王朝饭店
time-pressed	goouqiaang	够呛
to bank of china	quu zhonggguo yinnhanng	去中国银行
to save time	sheenng shhijian	省时间
to where	quu nnaar	去哪儿
today	jintian	今天
tomorrow	minngtian	明天
tomorrow okay	minngtian kkeeyyii ma?	明天可以吗？
too late	taai waann le	太晚了
tower	bbaaolleei	堡垒
Toy Department	Wannjuu Buuvhvjh	玩具部
trade	maaoyii	贸易
traffic	jiaotong	交通
train station is where	hhuooche zhaan zaai nnaar	火车 在哪儿
travel service	lleuuxinngshe	旅行社
troubling you	mmafann ninn	麻烦您
tung-an market	dong an shiichaanng	东安市场
tutor	jiaaoshi	教师
Twenty-First Century Hotel	Eershhiyih Shiijii Faandiaan	二十一世纪饭店
U u	*[Linear Script]*	*[Square Script]*
unification	toonngyihuaa	统一化
Union Medical College Hospital	Bbeeijing Xxiehhe Yiyuaan	北京协和 医院
unsafe	buu anquannde	不 安全的
urban	chenngshii	乘势
use elevator	yoong diaanti	用电梯
usually	jingchanng	经常
V v	*[Linear Script]*	*[Square Script]*
very	feichanng	非常

INTERNET-ENGLISH	INTERNET-CHINESE	CHINESE CHARACTERS
very big	heenn daa	很大
very expensive	heenn guii	很贵
very far	heenn yuaann	很远
very many days	heenn duo tian	很多天
visit	canguan	参观
visiting	yyoulaann	游览
W w	*[Linear Script]*	*[Square Script]*
wait a moment	shaoh deenng	稍 等
wait for me	deenng wwooj	等我
wait for two hours	deenng liaanng gee xxiaaoshhi	等两个小时
waiting for you	deenng ninn	等您
Wangfujing	Wanng Ffuuvhj Jiinng	王府井
want	yaao	要
warlords	junffa	军阀
wedding	hunllii	婚礼
welcome	huanyinng	欢迎
western	xifangde	西方的
western medicine	yoong xiyih	用西医
what	shennme	甚么
what sense	shennme yiisi	甚么意 思
what is	shennme shii	甚么是
what is that	nnaa shii shennme	哪是甚么
what is this	zhee shii shennme	这是甚么
what time	shennme shhihoou	甚么时候
what year	nnaa niann	哪年
where	nnaar	哪儿
where	shennme diifang	甚么地方
which floor	nnaa cenng llou	哪层楼
white rice	bbaifaan	白饭
who	shhei	谁
why	weeishennme	为甚么
why so	hheguu	何故

INTERNET-ENGLISH	INTERNET-CHINESE	CHINESE CHARACTERS
wife	qizi	妻子
winds-waters [feng shui]	fengshhuii	风水
worth	jiaazhhi	价值
written	xxieede	写的
X x	*[Linear Script]*	*[Square Script]*
Xerox	Ganyiin	干印
xylophone	muuqinn	木琴
Y y	*[Linear Script]*	*[Square Script]*
yes	shiide	是的
you keep the change	ninn shou xiaa linngqiann	您收下零钱
you like	nniiy xxiihuan	你喜欢
you, very kind	ninn zhen hhaao	您真好
your	nniide	你的
your suggestions	nniide jiaanyii	你的建议
Z z	*[Linear Script]*	*[Square Script]*
zoological park	doongwuu yuannlph	动物园

田™ TiENSTROKES ® USA
www. internetchinese.com * China Certificate of Standardization®1999 * www.tienstrokes.com

ADDRESSES in Beijing	DIIZHHII zaai Bbeeijing	地址在北京
NATIONS' NAMES (EMBASSIES' ADDRESSES IN BEIJING)	GGUOMINNG (DAASHHIIGUAANN DIIZHHII ZAAI BBEEIJING)	国名 (大使馆 地址)
ENGLISH	INTERNET-CHINESE	SINOGRAPHS
Algeria	AhEerrJjiLiiYaa (San Llii Tunn 21 Haao Llou)	阿尔及利亚 (三里屯21号楼)
Argentina	AhGenTinng (San Llii Tunn 31 Haao Llou)	阿根廷 (三里屯31号楼)
Australia	AaoDaaLiiYaa (Dong Zhhi Menn Waai Daajie)	澳大利亚 (东直门外大街)
Brazil	BaXi (Jiaangguo Menn Waai Guang Hhuajljc Luu)	巴西 (建国门外光华路)
Britain	Yinggguo (Guang Hhuajljc Luu 5 Haao)	英国(光华路5号)
Canada	Jianadaa (Dong Zhhi Menn Waai Daajie)	加拿大 (东直门外大街)
Chile	Zhiilii (San Llii Tunn 22 Haao Llou)	智利 (三里屯22号楼)
France	Ffaagguo (San Llii Tunn Dong San Jie)	法国 (三里屯东三街)
Germany	Ddegguo (Dong Zhhi Menn Waai Daajie)	德国 (东直门外大街)
Hungary	Xiongjp Yya Liilj (San Llii Tunn 17 Haao Llou)	匈牙利 (三里屯17号楼)
India	Yiinduu (Guang Hhuajljc Luu 8 Haao)	印度(光华路8号)
Iran	Yilaanng (San Llii Tunn 36 Haao Llou)	伊朗 (三里屯36号楼)
Japan	Riibeenn (Jiaangguo Menn Waai Rii Tannhlt Luu)	日本(建国门外日坛路)
Korea	Chhaoxian (Rii Tannhlt Bbeei Luu)	朝鲜 (日坛北路)
Palestine	Baleesitaann (Dong Zhhi Menn Waai Daajie)	巴勒斯坦(东直门外大街)
Russia	EhhLluoSi (Dong Zhhi Men Neei Dong Zhong Jiejjl)	俄罗斯 (东直门内东中街)
Thailand	Taaigguo (Jiaangguo Menn Waai Guang Hhuajljc Luu)	泰国 (建国门外光华路)
United States of America	Mmeeigguo (Jiaangguo Menn Waai Xiuujtv Shhuii Bbeei Jiejjl)	美国(建国门外秀水北街)

PLACES & ADDRESSES INTERNET-ENGLISH	DIIFANG & DIIZHHII INTERNET-CHINESE	地方&地址 方块-汉字
Beijing Branch	Bbeeijing Fensheejv	北京分社
Beijing Foreign Trade Bureau	Bbeeijing Shiwaai Maaoyii	北京市外贸易
Beijing Public Security Bureau, Foreign Affairs Section	Bbeeijing Shiivh GongAn Jju, Waaishii Ke	北京市公安局,外事科
Beijing Railway Station	Bbeeijing Hhuooche Zhaanvhv	北京火车站
Beijing West Railway Station	Bbeeijing Hhuooche Xih Zhaanvhv	北京火车西站
Booking Office	Shooujlv Piaao Chuu	售票处
CAAC	ZhongGguo Minnhanng Zoonngjju	中国民航总局
Capital Airport	Shhooudu Jichaanng	首都机场
Chairman Mao Memorial Hall	Mmao Zhhuuxxi Jiiniaan Tanng	毛主席记念堂
China Arts and Crafts Import and Export Corporation	ZhongGguo Gongyii Piinn Jiinchu Kkoou Zoonng Gongsi	中国工艺品进出口总公司
China International Travel Service	ZhongGguo Gguojii Lleuuxinngshe	中国国际旅行社
China National Cereals, Oils and Foodstuffs Import and Export Corporation	ZhongGguo Lianngyyou Shhipiinn Jiinchu Kkoou Zoonng Gongsi	中国粮油食品进出口总公司
China National Light Industrial Products Import and Export Corporation	Qinghcl Gongyee Jiinchu Kkoou Zoonng Gongsi	中国轻功业进出口总公司
China National Machinery Import and Export Corporation	ZhongGguo Jixiee Jiinchu Kkoou Zoonng Gongsi	中国机械进出口总公司
China National Native Produce and Animal By-Products Import and Export Corporation	ZhongGguo Ttuuchaann Chuuvh Jiinchu Kkoou Gongsi	中国土产畜进出口公司
China Stamps Import and Export Company	Yyoupiaao Jiinchu Kkoou Gongsi	邮票进出口公司
Dong-Dan Post Office	Dong-Dan Yyoujju	东-单邮局
Foreign Languages Press	Waaiwenn Chubaann Shee	外文出版社
Government Offices & Enterprises	Jiguan & Qqiiyee	机关&企业
Hsin Hwa (New China) News Agency	XinHhuaShee (XinHhua XinwennShee)	新华社 (新华新闻社)

Office of the General Administration of Customs	Hhaaiguan Zoonngshhuu Daallou	海关总署大楼
Telegraph Building	Diaanbaao Daallou	电报大楼
The Great Hall of the People	Rennminn Daahuii Tanng	人民大会堂
The Ministry of Foreign Affairs	Waaijiao Buuvh	外交部
The Ministry of Foreign Trade	Waaimaao Buuvh	外贸部
DIPLOMATIC APARTMENT	WAAIJIAO GONGYUU	外交公寓
Apartment for Diplomatic Personnel at Chi Chia Yuan	Jjivh Jiavvp Yuannlph Waaijiao Gongyuu	齐家园外交公寓
Apartment for Diplomatic Personnel at San Li Tun	San Llii Tunn Waaijiao Gongyuu	三里屯外交公寓
Diplomatic Office Building at San Li Tun	San Llii Tunn Waaijiao Baangong Daallou	三里屯外交办公大楼
New Apartment outside Chienkoumen	Jiaangguo Mennwaai Waaijiao Gongyuu	建国门外外交公寓
HOTELS	LLEUUGUAANN	旅馆
21st Century Hotel	Eer Shhi Yih Shiijii Faandiaan	二十一世纪饭店
Asia Hotel Beijing	Yaazhou Daa Jjiuudiaann	亚洲大酒店
Beijing Hilton Hotel	Xijyh Eerrj Duunhcl Faandiaan	希尔顿饭店
Beijing Hotel	Bbeeijing Faandiaan	北京饭店
Continental Grand Hotel	Wwuuzhou Daa Jjiuudiaan	五洲大酒店
CVIK Hotel	Saai Tee Faandiaan	赛特饭店
Dioayutai State Guest House	Diaaoyyu Ttai Gguo Binguaann	钓鱼台国宾馆
Friendship Hotel	Yyoouyii Faandiaan	友谊饭店
Gloria Plaza Hotel	Kkaailcl Caai Daa Jjiuudiaan	凯莱大酒店
Grand Hotel Beijing	Guiibin Llou Faandiaan	贵宾楼饭店
Great Wall Hotel	Channg Chennghlt Faandiaan	长城饭店
Holiday Crown Plaza	Huanngguan Jiaarii Faandiaan	皇冠假日饭店
Holiday Inn Downtown Beijing	Jin Du Jiaarii Faandiaan	金都假日饭店
Holiday Inn Lido Beijing	Liidu Jiaarii Faandiaan	丽都假日饭店
Hsiang Shan Hotel	Xiang Shan Faandiaan	香山饭店
International Hotel	Gguojii Faandiaan	国际饭店
Jingguang New World Hotel	Jing Guaanng Zhongxin	京广中心
Kempinski Hotel	KaiBinSiJi [Kailcl Bin Sihllh Jihllh] Faandiaan	凯宾斯基饭店
Kunlun Hotel	Kunlunn Faandiaan	昆仑饭店
Landmark Hotel	Liaang Mmaa Faandiaan	亮马饭店
Nationalities Hotel	Minnzzu (Min Tzu) Faandiaan	民族饭店

New Otani Chang Fu Gong Hotel	Channg Fuuvvp Gongvvp Faandiaan –	长富宫饭店
Novotel	Song Heevpj Daa Jjiuudiaan	松鹤大酒店
Olympic Hotel	Aaohy Linn Ppii Keehl Faandiaan	奥林匹克饭店
Palace Hotel	Wanng Ffuuvhj Faandiaan	王府饭店
Peace Hotel	Hhepinng Binguaann	和平宾馆
Poly Plaza	Bbaao Liijhl Daashaa	保利大厦
Shangrila Hotel Beijing	Xiang Llii La Faandiaan	香格里拉饭店
Swissotel	Gaanngvvt Aaovvt Zhongxin Ruiihhl Shiihlh Faandiaan	港澳中心瑞士饭店
Tianlun Dynasty Hotel	Tian Lunn Wanngchhao Faandiaan	天仑王朝饭店
SHOPS & RESTAURANTS	**SHANGDIAAN & CANTING**	商店&餐厅
Beijing Duck Restaurant Outside Chien-men	Bbeeijing Kkaaoya Diaanvhj	北京烤鸭店
Beijing Paintings Shop	Bbeeijing Huaah Diaanvhj	北京画店
China Arts Saloon	ZhongGguo Yiitt Yuaantt	中国艺苑
Cultural Relics Shop	Wennwuu Shangdiaan	文物商店
Curios Shop	Jjis Gguuhllph Ggevlp	汲古阁
Department Store	Bbaaihuoo Daallou	百货大楼
Friendship Store	Yyoouyii Shangdiaan	友谊商店
Jung Pao Chai	Ronnghll Bbaao Zhaivhjy	荣保斋
Kaorou Wan Restaurant	Kkaaoroou Yuaanhll	烤肉苑
Liulichang Street	Lliulli Chaanng Jiejjl	琉璃厂街
Tingliguan Restaurant	Ting Llijpvzh Guaannjpg Faanzhuang	听鹂馆饭庄
Tung-An Market	Dong An Shiichaanng	东安市场
Tunghojun Ji Restaurant	Kkaaoroou Jiijhljy	烤肉季
Yanjing Studio	Yaanhllh Jingvh Shuhuaa Sheevplv	燕京书画社
HISTORICAL SITES & PLACES OF RECREATION	**MINNGSHEENG GGUUJI & YYULEE CHAANNGSSUOO**	名胜古迹&娱乐场所
Altar of the Earth	DiiTann	地坛
Altar of the Moon	Yueetann	月坛
Altar of the Sun	Riitann	日坛
Beihai North Sea Park	Bbeeihhaai Gongyuannjl	北海公园
Beijing Zoo	Bbeeijing Doongwuu Yuannlph	北京动物园
Chungshan Park	Zhongshan Gongyuannjl	中山公园
Hsiang Shan Park	Xiangshan Gongyuannjl	香山公园
Marco Polo Bridge	Lluhll Gouvvt Qqiaohlj	芦沟桥
Ming Tombs	Minng Chhao Shhisan Linng	明朝十三陵
Museum of Nature	Ziirann Bbowuu Guaannjpg	自燃博物馆

Purple Bamboo Park	Zziilhl Zhhu Yuannzl Gongyuannjl	紫竹园公园
Scenic Hills Park	Jiinnglph Shan Gongyuannjl	景山公园
Temple of the Sleeping Buddha	Woohlphlc Ffojl Sihlh	卧佛寺
The Cultural Palace of the Nationalities	Minnzzu Wennhuaa Gongvvp	民族文化宫
The Great Wall	Channg Chennghlt	长城
The Military Museum of Chinese Revolution	ZhongGguo Ggemiing Jun Shiih Bbowuu Guaannj	中国革命军事博物馆
The Museum of Chinese History	ZhongGguo Liishhii Bbowuu Guaannj	中国历史博物馆
The Museum of Chinese Revolutionary History	ZhongGguo Ggemiing Liishhii Bbowuu Guaannj	中国革命历史一一物馆
The National Art Gallery	ZhongGguo Mmeeishuu Guaannjpg	中国美术馆
The Palace Museum	Guugong Bbowuu Guaannjpg	故宫博物馆
The Summer Palace	Yyihll Hhe Yuannlph	颐和园
The Temple of Heaven	Tiantann Gongyuannjl	天坛公园
Tiananmen	Tian An Menn	天安门
Working People's Place of Culture	Llaodoong Rennminn Wennhuaa Gongvvp	劳动人民文化宫
PLACES OF RECREATION & MORE HISTORICAL SITES	YYULEE CHAANNGSSUOO & FUUJIA MINNGSHEENG GGUUJI	娱乐场所&附加名胜古迹
Beijing Television	Bbeeijing Diaanshii Ttai	北京电视台
Capital Cinema	Shhooudu Diaanyiinng Yuaanzl	首都电影院
Celestial Bridge Theater	Tian Qqiaohljv Juuchaanng	天桥剧场
Central Broadcasting and Television Transmission Tower	Zhongyang Diaanshii Ttai	中央电视台
Hsien Non Tan Stadium	Xian Nonng Tannhlt Ttiiyuu Chaanngth	先农坛体育场
Monument to the People's Heroes	Rennminn Yingxionng Jiiniaan Beihj	人民英雄记念碑
National Olympic Sports Center	Gguojia Aolinpike (Olympic)Ttiiyuu Zhongxin	国家奥林匹克体育中心
The Beijing Gymnasium	Bbeeijing Ttiiyuu Guaannjpg	北京体育馆
The Beijing Workers' Gymnasium	Bbeeijing Gongrenn Ttiiyuu Guaannjpg	北京工人体育馆
The Beijing Workers' Stadium	Bbeeijing Gongrenn Ttiiyuu Chaanngth	北京工人体育场
The Capital Gymnasium	Shhooudu Ttiiyuu Guaannjpg	首都体育馆
The Capital Theater	Shhooudu Juuchaanng	首都剧场

The International Club	Gguojii Juulee Buuvh	国际俱乐部
The Theater of the Beijing Exhibition Center	Bbeeijing Zhaannlaann Guaannjpg Juuchaanng	北京展览馆剧场
Yanhuang Museum	Yannvk Huanng Yiishuu Guaannjpg	炎黄艺术馆
HOSPITALS	YIYUAAN	医院
Beijing Maternity Hospital	Bbeeijing Fuuchaann Yiyuaan	北京妇产医院
Beijing Stomatology Hospital	Bbeeijing Kkoouqiang Yiyuaan	北京口腔医院
Beijing Tongren Hospital	Bbeeijing Tonngrenn Yiyuaan	北京同仁医院
Beijing Union Medical College Hospital	Bbeeijing Xxiehhe Yiyuaan	北京协和医院
Chi Shui Tan Hospital	Jijtv shhuii Yiyuaan	积水医院
Children's Hospital	Errtonng Yiyuaan	儿童医院
China-Japan Friendship Hospital	Zhong-Rii Yyoouhhaao Yiyuaan	中-日友好医院
Emergency Phone: 120	Jjijiuu Diaanhuaa: 120	急救电话:120
International Medical Center	Gguojii Yilliaao Zhongxin	国际医疗费中心
TEMPLES & CHURCHES	SIIMIAAO & JIAAOTANNG	寺庙＆教堂
Catholic Church	Tianzhhuu Jiaaotanng	天主教堂
Christian Church	Yesu Jiaaotanng	耶苏教堂
Mosque	Qingzhen Siith	清真寺
Temple of Azure Clouds	Biihhl Yunn Siith	碧云寺
The Temple of Reclining Buddha	Woolv Ffojl Siith	卧佛寺
Yonghe Palace (a Lama Temple)	Yongvh Hhe Gongvvp	雍和宫

BEIJING COMPUTER-CHINESE PROJECT

拼写汉字键盘输入法
北京试验班总结报告
(1995 年 7 月修订稿)

BEIJING PINXXIEE REPORT
北京 拼写 报告
BBEEIJING PINXXIEE BAAOGAAO

Results Of Beijing Pinxxiee Experimental Class Final Report

[Written, revised and translated, 1995-1997]

By

Huang Zongxuan, First Educational Consultant, Editor
(Huanng Zongvvp Xuannvjjv, 黄宗煊)
Lin Jianxiang, Computer-aided Instruction (CAI) Consultant
(Linn Jiaanphh Xianngvplv, 林建祥)
Zhang Zimeng, Pinxxiee Project Teacher, Drafter
Zhangphz Zzii Meengjhhhg, 张 子锰
Wang Yang, Pinxxiee Project Teacher, Drafter
(Wanng Yannglphh, 王 日易)
Gareth Roberts Tien, Translator
田一泽
Tiann Yih Zzes

Tiann San Wenn, Tenstrokes Pinxxiee Consultant, TransEditor

(This report was initiated by the Pinxxiee Experimental Class teacher Zhang Zimeng (Huiwen High School Computer Room Teacher), and Instructor Wang Yang (Jingshan High School Language Room Teacher). The teachers wrote the first draft for evaluation and appraisal and submitted it to Mr. Huang Zongxuan, Cadre of Commission of Education of the People's Republic of China. Mr. Huang was the person in charge of the Pinxxiee experiment (contributed time and planning, while on leave from the Commission). Mr. Huang wrote and expanded the final version in consultation of Professor Lin Jianxiang, Vice Chairman of All China Computer-aided Instruction Association. Professor Lin also served as CAI consultant of the Pinxxiee Experimental Class Project in Beijing. The Chinese report was translated into English by Gareth R. Tien. Finally, Dr. H. C. Tien (Tiann San Wenn) served as TransEditor and reviewed, edited, and rendered the final report in 3 scripts, Pinxxiee, Chinese characters and English letters.)

ABSTRACT

Experimental Results and Appraisal

This was the first sponsored experiment of the Pinxxiee input system in the PRC. Because of time limitations and lack of experience, the experiments were not planned and organized to its perfection. None the less, under the support and direction of the pertinent government bodies and school principals, as well as nearly 200 students along with their instructors, et al, earnestly endeavored to work on the project. During the project, many students arrived early at their schools to practice on the computers. Still others did not tarry during the lessons. They even stayed after class to practice on the computers. Nightly, the teachers prepared the lessons. They too practiced on the computers. For these above reasons, the project was a success. Fundamentally, the purpose of the project was achieved.

Based on the aforementioned Pinxxiee Method Introduction, the experiment conditions, its results, the teachers' responses, and the reference manual entitled <u>Chinese Character Input Keyboard Technology and Theory</u>, we have the following evaluation of Pinxxiee Input Method's ease of learning and speed of input:

A. **Criteria for Judging the Ease of Learning a Chinese Character Input System:**

In the aforementioned reference publication, "The criteria for judging ease of learn a Chinese character input system is determined by the following considerations: (1) The user knows approximately 3,000 Chinese characters; (2) The user knows pinyin; Chinese multi-character words can be looked up by using radicals; characters can be written using the correct stroke order. China's textbooks already contain these criteria." The publication also points out: "The pinyin based methods.... nearly all do not need additional information to memorize".

The complete pinyin spelling input method for Chinese Characters requires the least memorizing effort in the three aspects of characteristic information structure, information coding procedures and the reflection of coding elements and key elements, so it is an easy-to-learn input method. For the phonetic-graphic input methods, with phonetic as primary and graphic as supplement, the main effort of memorizing goes to the graphical coding part. By comparison, radical formation input method (including structure part) requires long term and much bigger memory capacity. Therefore, it is not easy to learn.

Based on the above theoretical point, we can clearly see that Pinxxiee, being totally based on pinyin, is easy to learn and use by primary school students. Having learned pinyin, students only need to practice for a week and learn the following: 1) pinyin plus tones, 2) Tenstrokes. After practicing continuously for a period 60 to 70 silent radicals, they will be able to handle 95% of common characters. As for adults who have mastered pinyin, the same conditions apply to them for learning Pinxxiee.

B. **Regarding Tenstrokes Input Speed**

According to the aforementioned reference manual: "Most people using Chinese character word processors (that is non-professional typists) are more concerned with ease of use rather than speed." "Most non-professional typists are satisfied with typing 15 - 30 words per minute."

For various reasons, this test classes' input speed was not high. The average was 8 characters per minute. Analyzing the tests showed three problems: 1) A portion of the students had not mastered sufficiently pinyin;

A portion of the students were not familiar with using the keyboard; 3) The Pinxxiee character spellings are on the average longer than other character representations. Nonetheless, there were students at similar levels of educational backgrounds, which produced the following results. Beijing University's No. 2 Elementary School performed twice and thrice as fast as Beijing University's Elementary and Chongwen Elementary Schools, respectively.

Furthermore, Beijing University's No. 2 Experimental Elementary School had one student who achieved typing 42 characters per minute, attaining the honor role. In addition, there were 2 students who achieved 21-26 characters per minute; and 7 students achieved 10 -17 characters per minute. Of other elementary schools' experimental classes, 20% on average typed 10 characters per minute or more.

We can predict that had this experiment been organized over a period of 6 complete days, the students would have been more completely adapted to Pinxxiee. Thus, the students' input speed for sure would have increased to 15 - 30 characters per minute.

At present, Dr. Tien is making adjustments to the software based on students' and teachers' reactions. He is prepared to produce a Chinese version with phrase input and speed codes for Pinxxiee (with a goal of 100 characters per minute) in version PX2001 v2.0. At this time, it would become possible for Beijing's high schools and elementary schools to test and use the software.

C. Regarding the Future of Pinxxiee's Use and Proliferation

During the month of November 1994, the Vice-Director of the Chinese National Committee, Dong Fang Zeng, met with Dr. Tien. He listened to a detailed explanation of the Pinxxiee input method from Dr. Tien and watched a presentation of the software. Minister of Electronics, Hu Qi Li, and Director of the Ministry's Computer Software Division, Chen Chong, both listened to Dr. Tien's presentation. In January of 1995, China's Chinese Language Association's Director; Chinese Engineering scholar, Chen Li Wei; China's National Education Committee's Vice Director, Liu Bin also met with Dr. Tien and watched the demonstration. They very much admired and approved of Dr. Tien's more than 20 years of spirited in-depth Pinxxiee research. Furthermore, they felt that Pinxxiee had value in educational research in China's elementary and high schools. This past experiment was conducted under their authority with their special organizing. Therefore, the Pinxxiee method can be one of those being used in the near future (within this millennium's last five years) at designated times and placed elementary schools. In this way we can greatly spread pinyin and popularize Mandarin; and moreover, spread the use of computers in meeting with the 21st Century information age.

From a long-term viewpoint, the Pinxxiee input method could be aligned to be used on the "Information Superhighway". Because of the aforementioned explanation, Pinxxiee's use can aide the people of China to copy the people of the Western world, and have the spoken language and written language united on one keyboard using letters to input. "And because at this time there is no popularly used input method which is alphabetic, let alone is not a language, we have no system that can be read by people. These systems can only be read as computer codes." (The above quote is from Chinese Computer World Magazine.) Nonetheless, Pinxxiee Input Method is at the same time both Chinese character input and Mandarin language input. Its input is readable Mandarin Chinese; its output is ancient, beautiful Chinese characters. The two co-exist, being able to switch one to the other simultaneously. If users are working on a multi-computer network, is it possible that they can both type Chinese characters and read Pinxxiee as written Chinese? Yes, of course. We want to achieve this ideal; at the same time, there exist a number of technical problems that need to be discussed and overcome. In the aforementioned magazine,

Chinese Computer World, the article states, "Chinese character input method is the most important thing China's computer industry today. .... If a kind of character input method easy to learn and fast to use; furthermore, has wide reaching acceptance, and therefore has great usefulness". The Pinxxiee input method can possibly become that ideal method the Chinese people have sought for. No matter what, Dr. Tien's nearly 30 year's of arduous research already have shown that the use of the international keyboard has realized Premiere Zhou En Lai's goal: "The pinyin method (excluding the tones) still can be used to write Chinese characters. It can serve as an effective tool for studying Mandarin Chinese." "It can also serve as a tool to for teaching non-native speakers of Chinese and thus help to build a cultural bridge between east and west." (See Zhou En Lai Educational Article, pp. 172 -173 'Modern Day Chinese Character Reform').

(This report was written in Chinese square characters [方块汉字] by experimental class teacher Zhang Zi Meng (Huiwen High School Computer Room Teacher), Instructor Wang Yang (Jingshan High School Language Teacher); they wrote the first draft. The later revisions were done by the person in charge of the experiment, the China National Committee retiree cadre, Huang Zong Xuan (Huanng Zongv Xuanv); Chinese National Computer Assistant Director, experimental class consultant, Prof. Lin Jian Xiang (Linn Jiaanp Xianngv);   Dr. Tien approved the final draft. Translation by Gareth Roberts Tien 田一泽 Tiann Yih Zzes , 1996.)

中国标准化协会文件

中标协发秘字[1990]032 号
CHINA STANDARDIZATION ASSOCIATION DOCUMENT
CSA CONFIDENTIAL CODE [1990] No 032▯

November 5, 1999, Beijing, People's Republic of China
CONCLUSION REPORT
By Panel of Experts at China Standardization Conference
On PINXXIEE Language Technology
By Dr. H. C. Tien (Tiann San Wenn, 田 三 文)

CERTIFICATE OF AUTHENTICATION

The China Standardization Association hereby decrees that the Panel of Experts was indeed authorized to review Dr. H. C. Tien's (Tiann San Wenn, 田三文博士) presentation and demonstration in defense of his Pinxxiee Language Technology. Furthermore, this conference was declared on public record that the expert panel's conclusions are true and valid.

On November 3, 1999, a conference was held in Beijing, China, at which Dr. H. C. Tien demonstrated and defended his Pinxxiee Language Technology. The technology was subsequently validated by the China Standardization Association (CSA). The CSA invited China's experts and authorities in the following fields to participate in the review process: information technology, standardization, ergonomics, software engineering, software design, language coding analysis, psychology, Internet technology analysis, and allied fields.

The following conclusions were reached by the Panel of Experts and confirmed by the Association.

1. Pinxxiee Language Technology was developed based on the Chinese Government's official standards of spoken Mandarin and the Chinese ("Pinyin") phonetic spelling method. Moreover, this technology adheres to the contents of China's official Mandarin language _Xinhua Dictionary_. In conclusion this language technology's overall design is in accordance with China's national Mandarin language policies.
2. This technology is an effective system of writing Chinese characters because the problem of duplicate Chinese character spellings is rendered small. All aspects of a Chinese character -- i.e. the phonetic spelling, tone, and semantic root -- are expressed in its Pinxxiee language spelling.
3. This technology is a breakthrough in solving the problem of homophone ambiguity in Mandarin because Pinxxiee spells out all aspects of the Chinese character (see above point # 2). For all practical purposes, the homophone problem has been solved.
4. Pinxxiee Language Technology is in ASCII, so it can be used on the Internet to send Chinese Mandarin email messages (as easily as in English) without the ambiguity that arises when the phonetic "Pinyin" spelling method is used. Thus, fluent speakers of Mandarin, who do not know English and do not have a Chinese character platform on their PC, now have a convenient method for sending and receiving email messages in Mandarin Chinese. This is

especially true for international communication, and will have ever increasing usefulness in the future.

5. There is sufficient education software available for Pinxxiee Language Technology, and the PX-2001 software package (PX Toolbox) makes learning this technology easy.

In summary, Pinxxiee Language Technology's method of spelling Chinese characters is technically sound; it has simple rules and very little memorizing needed for the tones in Mandarin Chinese, the standard spoken language of People's Republic. It is suitable for being introduced for learning as early as the elementary and junior high school grade levels by students who have knowledge of China's Pinyin (Latin letters) spelling scheme.

The China Standardization Association hereby decrees that the Panel of Experts was indeed authorized to review Dr. H. C. Tien's presentation and demonstration in defense of his Pinxxiee Language Technology. Furthermore, China Standardization Association published the content of this conference on public record and declared the conclusions by the Panel Experts, valid.

The Signatures of Panel Experts of the Beijing Confirmation Conference Report on PINXXIEE THESIS is listed as follows:

Shi Yuncheng (Shhihj Yunn Chenngjh 石云程), Chief Engineer, PLA 2nd Armory Division, 2nd Research Institute

Wang Lijian (Wanng Liijhl Jiaanjyh 王利剑), Director, China Information Technology Standardization Commission

Liu Bisong (Lliuvhjy Biihhlt Song, 刘碧松) Divisional Director, China Standardization & Information Categorical Coding Research Institute

Fan Chenchen (Fannhljy Chenlphh Chenlphh, 樊晨晨), Ministry of Education Information Center

Tang Mingduan (Tangvvt Minngjh Duanvh, 汤铭端), Vice Director, Science Commission, China Aeronautics Ministry 204 Research Institute (overseas on assignment)

Zheng Renjie (Zheengvj Renn Jjiehljy, 郑人杰), Professor, Qinghhua University Software Center

Liu Qiyuan (Lliuvhjy Qqiivphj Yuannhj, 刘启原), Assistant Chief Engineer, Sinosoft Corporate Headquarters

Huang Jinjian (Huanng Jinjy Jiaanphh, 黄金建), Vice Director, China Standard Intelligence Research Institute Department of Research (absent on assignment)

Chen Yifan (Chenn Yih Fann, 陈一凡), Divisional Director, Information Engineering Institute

Ma Lincong (Mmaa Linn Conghllh, 马林聪), Secretary General, China Standardization Association

Xiao Hui (Xiaolvj Huiihlp, 肖惠), Vice Director, China Standardization & Information & Information Categorical Coding Research Institute

Yao Xiaojing (Yyaocjh Xxiaaolphh Jiinghhlh, 姚晓静) Senior Engineer, China Standard Intelligence Research Institute Department of Research

[Abridged English translation version by Gareth R. Tien 田一泽 **Tiann Yih Zzes:**
see full original document on www.internetchinese.com]

PROMOTION AND POPULARIZATION

Peking Pinxxiee Group Announcement

PINXXIEE CORPORATION has worked steadily to promote the use of <u>TiENSTROKES Alphabet Chart</u> and the <u>Internet-Chinese Script</u> on the Internet (1983-2001). The Internet-Chinese Pinxxiee products are now (2002) available on the web at www.internetchinese.com .

Our company has specially designed the TaxiTutor: Mandarin-Chinese Language Companion in an Airport Version for tourists and a Classroom Tutorial for teachers and students. An audiocassette of both English and Mandarin-Chinese is available, for Chinese to learn English and English-speaking people to learn to speak Chinese. The audiocassette provides 10 basic lessons of commonly used phrases for beginners. These 10 basic lessons are included in the TaxiTutor in 3 scripts: English, Internet-Chinese and Chinese characters. The same pages of the 10 basic lessons are also on the above website.

China Standardization Expert Panel noted that Mandarin-Chinese speakers now have a direct and faster method of spelling <u>Pinyin *with tone-letters*</u>, to send and receive e-mail messages in the linearized Mandarin-Chinese script, just like English on the Net. And English speakers can also learn to read, spell Mandarin, and e-mail conveniently and more accurately in Chinese.

Since Standardization (1999), CCC Pinxxiee Company has received and is continuously receiving positive support from Peking University Group with its associate Elementary School and other Beijing elementary schools, including Peking University Experimental School. This standardized Internet-Chinese Pinxxiee tutorial program was presented in GCCCE-2000, Singapore. It is now on the website of Peking University Elementary School: www.bdfx.net.cn.

CCC has also received positive feedback regarding the use of Pinxxiee Internet-Chinese language technology in Hunan, Hubei, Guizhou and other provincial elementary and high schools. Plans are being considered to establish Internet-Chinese educational centers in Shanghai, Nanjing and other areas, e.g. Hong Kong, in order to link with Internet-Chinese educational centers in Michigan, New York, California, Washington and other states in U.S.A; as well as in the city of Toronto and the provinces of Canada.

The Peking Pinxxiee Group is currently accepting applications from educators worldwide, and especially welcomes all GCCCE-2002 members to build Internet-Chinese Pinxxiee EduCenters via the Internet. For details, please first obtain a personal copy of <u>TaxiTutor:</u> <u>Mandarin-Chinese Language Companion</u> and/or contact the group liaison person, Professor Lin Jianxiang or Vice President Li Jianxin, at GCCCE-2002 Conference, Beijing, China.

THE PEKING PINXXIEE GROUP

Honorary Chairman: Ambassador Chai Zemin (Chhailhlh Zzevvt Minn, Daashhii, 柴泽民大使**)**
First Educational Consultant: Mr. Huang Zongxuan (Huanng Zong Xuanvjjv, Xs., 黄宗煊先生**)**

Professor Lin Jianxiang (Linn Jiaanphh Xianngvplv, Jiaaoshoou, 林建祥教授, 北京大学.**)**
Professor Tian Fangzeng (Tiann Fang Zenghlt, Jiaaoshoou, 田方增,教授, 中国科学院.**)**
Vice Principal Li Jianxing (Lliihljy Jiaanphh Xinvh, 李建新 校长,北大附属实验学校.**)**
Student Representative, Mr. Shi Weiping (Shhiilph Weeihll Pinng Xs. 史蔚平 先生, 北京联合大学.**)**
Software Engineer, Mr. Zhao Huixi (Zhaaohlh Huiih Xihl Xs., 赵惠熙 先生, **Toronto, Canada.)**

tsw ed., 2002-1-1

田 ™TiENSTROKES ® CHINESE COMPUTER COMMUNICATIONS (CCC), Inc.
TaxiTutor™

CAS CHINA ASSOCIATION FOR STANDARDIZATION 中國標準化協會	田™ CHINESE COMPUTER COMMUNICATIONS DIVISION of PINXXXIEE CORPORATION 中文電腦通訊一拼寫公司

Training Course for Internet-Chinese Character spelling
因 特 网 - 中 文 拼 写 技 术 培 训 研 讨 班

CERTIFICATE

证 书

Zheengshu

THIS is to certify that

PEKING UNIVERSITY ELEMENTARY SCHOOL*

has participated in the course held in Beijing on Nov **3, 2000**.

2000 年 11 月 03 日參加了在北京舉行的因特網---中文拼寫技術

培訓研討班，特發此證。 03/11/2000 Canjiale zaai Bbeeijing

Jjuuxinngde YinTeeWaanng-Zhongwenn Pinxxiee Jiishuu Ppeixuun

Yannttaoban, Tee Fa Ccii Zheengvz. **Ggeei BbeeiDaa FuuXxiaao:**

  * Li Jianxin, 李建新, Lliihljy Jiaanphh Xinvhvjh, BDFX
  Director of Curriculum has since instituted Internet-Chinese
  Tutorial on school's website: www.bdfx.net.cn/new_page_18.htm

H.C.TiEN,MD President, CCC Division **PINXXXIEE** Corporation 田三文 Tiann San Wenn 拼写公司 总经理 Date: 03/11/2000	**MA LIN-CONG** Secretary-general of CAS 马林聪 Mmaa Linn Cong 中国标准化协会 秘书长 Date: 03/11/2000

110

INTERNATIONAL ENDORSEMENT OF
DR. TIEN &
WORLDWIDE ACCLAIM FOR THE DISCOVERY OF
TENSTROKES ® GLOBAL ALPHABET

* * * * *

H. C. Tien, M.D., "Alumni's invention bridges East and West…. a revolutionary word processing system he invented that adapts the Chinese language to a standard IBM-compatible personal computer."   -ADVANCE ALUMNI, UNIVERSITY OF MICHIGAN

"Dr. H. C. Tien, is a Beijing-born, U.S.-educated child psychiatrist - with added credentials in neurology and electrical engineering… this very combination of interests and expertise that helped the break through a translation barrier that has frustrated linguists and educators for centuries.
                                                                        -IBM OUTLOOK

"According to Karlgren, the dichotomy between Latin phonetic script and the Chinese ideographic script could never be overcome:" But, Dr. Tien's R&D on Pinyin+Pinxxiee (*pronounced pinshay, meaning phonics+graphics*) reached the opposite conclusion: "The Pinxxiee Theory is that every Chinese ideograph can be transformed into an equivalent alphabetic word with no ambiguity."
                                                            -COMPUTER MAGAZINE, IEEE

"Tien's work represents a major breakthrough that may have a far-reaching effect on China's economy and trade, as well as on its still untapped scientific and technological potential."
                                                    -WASHINGTON AND LEE UNIVERSITY

"Dr. Tien has spent three decades focused on language and the brain."
                                                            -DETROIT FREE PRESS

"Your [Pinxxiee] quality translation process was greatly appreciated… for GM of China."
                                                    -GM POWERTRAIN HEADQUARTERS

"Because of his intelligent and humorous style of speaking, Dr. Tien is well received by audiences."
                                                    -CHICAGO CHINESE TIMES

"First Dr. H. C. Tien invented a new phonetic method of writing Chinese in Roman letters. Now, the …work has attracted scientists and scholars… Thanks to an American psychiatrist, the world's most populous nation can enter the computer age."   -THE WASHINGTON POST

Prof . Lin Jianxiang, Prof. Cai Cuiping, and Prof. Dong Yinwu: "We agree Dr. Tien's software used as elementary school computer-aided educational tools is very valuable for popularization."
                                                    -PEKING UNIVERSITY LANGUAGE LAB

"Tiann San Wenn's Pinxxiee Language Technology of Tenstrokes Global Alphabet and its derived Internet-Chinese script works just like English script on the Web… is the unique breakthrough solution to the Chinese Homophone Enigma."
                                                    -CHINA STANDARDIZATION ASSOCIATION

"I predict Dr. Tien's more than two decades of profound ☜ research in Pinxxiee Computer-Chinese and his PX 2001 software will be used in Chinese schools and other widespread applications, contributing to China's modernization of education, international communications and future development."
                    -HON. CHAI ZEMIN, THE FIRST PRC AMBASSADOR TO THE USA

田 ™TiENSTROKES ® CHINESE COMPUTER COMMUNICATIONS (CCC), Inc.
TaxiTutor™ Classroom Version: Teacher's Edition

Dr. TiEN's #1 Mandarin-Chinese

TaxiTutor™

Is the leading Modern Tutorial, since the beautiful Chinese characters were first created 6,000 years ago, along the Yellow River. Now, you, too, can master Chinese graphics, phonics and tones, all with a single TiENSTROKES Alphabet!

TaxiTutor™ teaches you in 10 basic Mandarin lessons: to speak, read and write _faster, better_, and even e-mail in Internet-Chinese script _accurately,_ just like English!

English: 10 Basic Lessons	THE INTERNET-CHINESE™ SCRIPT Mandarin: 10 Jibeenn Keewenn	汉字:10基本 课文
1. Chinese Phonetic Alphabet	1. Zhongwenn Pinyin Ziimmuu	1. 中文 拼音 字母
2. Greetings	2. Weenhoou	2. 问候
3. Traveler's Phrases	3. Lleuuxinng Ccijuu	3. 旅行 词句
4. Questions & Answers	4. Xunnween Hhe Hhuidda	4. 询问 和 回答
5. Numbers	5. Shuuzii	5. 数字
6. Time And Dates	6. Shhijian Hhe Riichenng	6. 时间和日程
7. Money	7. Huoobii	7. 货币
8. Food And Drinks	8. Shhiwuu Hhe Yiinnliaao	8. 食物 和 饮料
9. Communications	9. Tongxiin	9. 通信
10. Chinese Graphic Alphabet	10. Zhongwenn Xiaangxinng Ziimmuu	10. 中文象形字母

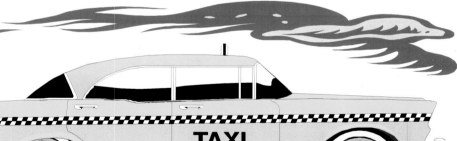

INTERNET-CHINESE PRESS, USA   **US$ 31.50**

Mandarin-Chinese Companion™
10 Basic TaxiTutor™ Lessons in
AudioCassette Available US $9.95

www.internetchinese.com

ISBN 0-9714824-2-X